BEST

FOR YOUR GARDEN

JANE HATTATT

This is a Parragon Book
This edition published in 2003

Parragon
Queen Street House
4 Queen Street
Bath BA1 1HE, UK

Conceived, edited, illustrated
and produced by Ditchfield Publishers

Cover Design by Bridgewater Books

ISBN 1-40540-478-7

A copy of the British Library Cataloguing in Publication
Data is available from the Library.

Typeset by Action Publishing Technology Ltd, Gloucester
Colour origination by Colour Quest Graghic Services Ltd,
London E9

Printed in China

Half title page: *Cistus purpureus*
Frontispiece: *Aconitum* 'Sparks's Variety'
Title page: *Alchemilla mollis* and *Nepeta X faassenii*
Contents page: *Hemerocallis* 'Bonanza'

CONTENTS

INTRODUCTION

ANYONE VISITING a nursery or garden centre today is likely to be confronted with a vast, if not bewildering, range of plants offered for sale. Making a choice is always difficult, no less so on account of the number of very tempting species and cultivars that are now readily available. Container grown plants, something which we all tend to take for granted, mean that it is possible to make purchases for the garden at almost any time of year for, unless the weather is particularly bad, planting is no longer restricted to autumn or spring. The problem that we all face is in deciding what to pile into the trolley and what must, sadly, be left on the sales benches.

Our final choice must always be dictated to a large degree by space and the conditions of our garden. It is as foolish to attempt to cultivate something which, within a short period of time, will outgrow its position as it is to plant a sun lover in shade or a lime hater in alkaline soil. Likewise a plant requiring the protection and shelter of a wall is unlikely to succeed in an exposed situation where, in all likelihood, it will be damaged by strong winds. Working with, rather than against, both soil and situation will result in plants that flourish and a garden which thrives.

SHRUBS AND TREES
Shrubs and trees form the backbone of any garden,

OPPOSITE: An inspired selection of border plants creating a tapestry effect.

A shrub with long-lasting blooms is an invaluable asset. This is *Cornus kousa chinensis*.

providing year-round structure and interest. Without them a garden may appear, however well planted, to lack emphasis. Of value throughout the seasons, they come into their own especially during the winter when many herbaceous plants have been cut to ground level. Their outline, etched against a winter sky, is a constant delight contributing much needed form and texture at a time which could otherwise seem a little dull. Furthermore, those trees and shrubs which boast interesting bark or possess coloured stems are an additional bonus, as are those which carry berries or, indeed, retain their leaves. Evergreen shrubs and trees should not be overlooked but care needs to be exercised when placing them in the garden. A good rule of thumb is to look upwards, to consider the skyline and see how, in maturity, they will relate to their surroundings. In form they are of greater substance than their deciduous cousins, the impact that they can make being all the greater and, therefore, possibly requiring more thought.

Where space is restricted, then choose those shrubs and trees which could be considered to have high performance value. It may be that in addition to attractive foliage, they flower and fruit. Perhaps they have especially good form, growing in a particularly pleasing manner. Maybe they possess good autumn colour, their foliage coming alive towards the year's end. Whatever, it is important to feel that they really earn a place in the garden and that they are an essential component of the overall design.

HERBACEOUS PERENNIALS

Herbaceous perennials, those plants which in the main die down and are dormant over winter, are the mainstay of the border from spring through until autumn. To these may be added bulbs, which are, in fact, simply bulbous perennials, and annuals, those plants which are grown mainly for flower colour and which are discarded at the end of the season. All of these give to the garden the colour which is so much enjoyed and admired as the year progresses. And there are, of course, perennials well suited to virtually any scheme or situation.

The arrangement of perennials within the border is a matter of personal choice and preference. Account will, obviously, need to be taken of plant size, any specific requirements, and the effect which is to be aimed for. Traditionally, taller growing perennials are placed towards the back of the border, the plants being graded downwards with the smallest ones at the front. Sometimes this pattern may be broken to advantage. To place tall plants at the front of the border, particularly those with thin stems which may, in effect, be seen through, is to create added interest and heightened awareness. It is a practice which, adopted from time to time, does away with any seeming monotony which may arise where a border is too ordered, too uniform. Some of the most pleasing results are to be obtained where blocks of plants of a single variety are placed together. Planted in groups of threes, fives, sevens or more where space allows, such an arrangement ensures flowers, and therefore interest, over a long period. Occasionally the repetition of a single plant, a spot plant, or a group, serves to add unity to a scheme and assists in carrying the eye forwards.

As any gardener knows, much of the enjoyment of gardening is in experimentation. Placing together perennials, shrubs and trees in different combinations will result in any number of very different and unusual effects and it is these, over the passage of time, which will give to any garden its unique character and particular appeal.

OPPOSITE: The tall-growing, grey *Artemisia ludoviciana* 'Valerie Finnis' sits in the front of a border so that you look through it to the contrasting foliage of *Achillea grandifolia*.

The best plants demand bold plantings, as here in a part of the author's garden.

HOW TO USE THIS BOOK

Approximate measurements of a plant's height and spread or just height are given in both metric and imperial measures. The height is the first measurement, as in for example 1.2m × 60cm/4 × 2ft. However, both height and spread vary so greatly from garden to garden since they depend on soil, climate, pruning and position (a plant grown in a container may well have its growth restricted), that these measurements are offered as guides only. This is especially true of trees and shrubs where ultimate growth can be unpredictable.

The following symbols are also used:

○ = the plant thrives in or tolerates full sun.

◑ = thrives in or tolerates part-shade.

● = thrives in or tolerates full shade.

◊ = prefers well-drained soil.

◐ = prefers moist soil (the text will state if the plant requires good drainage as well as moist soil, as is often the case).

◆ = prefers wet soil.

E = the plant is evergreen.

LH = needs acid soil and is intolerant of lime.

❋❋❋ = the plant is fully hardy and can survive winters in temperate regions.

❋❋ = the plant is only frost-hardy, not fully hardy and it is likely it will need shelter and protection during winter in temperate regions.

❋ = the plant is tender (or half-hardy) and even in mild winter areas it may need protection to survive, or can be grown under glass.

POISONOUS PLANTS

In recent years, concern has been voiced about poisonous plants or plants which can cause allergic reactions if touched. The fact is that many plants are poisonous, some in a particular part, others in all their parts. For the sake of safety, it is always, without exception, essential to assume that no part of a plant should be eaten unless it is known, without any doubt whatsoever, that the plant or its part is edible and that it cannot provoke an allergic reaction in the individual person who samples it. It must also be remembered that some plants can cause severe dermatitis, blistering or an allergic reaction if touched, in some individuals and not in others. It is the responsibility of the individual to take all the above into account.

1.
SHRUBS and TREES

Abeliophyllum distichum

Flowering from late winter to early spring, this slow-growing shrub is an excellent addition to the winter border. The flowers, carried on bare wood, are white, opening from blush pink buds, and are delicately scented. A sunny, warm wall is an ideal situation for *A. distichum* in order to encourage abundant flowering.

Height × **spread:** 1.5 × 1.5m/5 × 5ft

Soil: Best grown in fertile, moist but well drained soil.

Position: Well suited to a position in full sun. Either grow as a specimen or place within a mixed or shrub border.

Care: No regular pruning required. Remove any dead, damaged or unwanted growth over winter. Keep well watered until established.

❍ 💧 ❄❄❄

Acer griseum: Paper bark maple

Copper-coloured, peeling bark makes this an outstanding
and desirable tree. The cut-leafed, maple foliage colours
from mid-green in spring and summer to magnificent
shades of flame in autumn whilst the bark positively
glows in the winter sun. Slow growing and of compact
habit, *A. griseum* is a perfect choice for the smaller
garden.

Height × spread: *7.5 × 6m/25 × 20ft*

Soil: Best grown in fertile, moist, neutral to acidic soil.

Position: Well suited to a position in sun or partial shade. Either grow
as a specimen or place within a mixed or shrub border.

Care: No regular pruning required. Remove any dead, damaged or
unwanted growth over winter. Keep well watered until established.

○ ◑ | ◊ | LH | ❋❋❋

Acer palmatum **f.** *atropurpureum*: Maple

A large shrub with splendid bronze-purple foliage throughout the growing season. In autumn the finely cut leaves turn a startling bright red giving a spectacular appearance to the late season garden. All the Japanese maples grow attractively but this form in maturity takes on a wonderfully gnarled appearance.

Height × spread: 4.5 × 4.5m/15 × 15ft

Soil: Best grown in fertile, moist, neutral to acidic soil.

Position: Well suited to a position in partial shade. Either grow as a specimen or place within a mixed or shrub border.

Care: No regular pruning required. Remove any dead, damaged or unwanted growth over winter. Keep well watered until established.

◑ ◐ LH ❄❄❄

Amelanchier lamarckii: Snowy mespilus

A small tree well deserving of a place in even the tiniest of gardens for its long season of interest. Masses of snowy white flowers are produced with copper foliage in spring, later to be followed by striking autumn colour and purple-black fruits. If only a single tree can be accommodated in the garden, then this will more than earn its place.

Height × spread: 10 × 12m/33 × 39ft

Soil: Best grown in fertile, moist but well drained soil.

Position: Well suited to a position in full sun but tolerant of some shade. Either grow as a specimen or place within a mixed or shrub border.

Care: No regular pruning required. Remove any dead, damaged or unwanted growth over winter. Keep well watered until established.

○ ◑ | ◓ | ❋❋❋

Aralia elata 'Variegata': Angelica tree

An impressive specimen shrub cultivated principally for its dramatically variegated foliage. The large, mid-green leaves, broadly edged in white, are formed in late spring and are followed by clusters of white flowers in late summer. Tiered growth, where both leaves and flowers are held elegantly on flat planes, adds distinction to any garden situation.

Height × spread: 3.5 × 3m/12 × 10ft

Soil: Best grown in fertile, moist but well drained soil.

Position: Well suited to a position in sun or partial shade. Either grow as a specimen or place within a mixed or shrub border.

Care: No regular pruning required. Remove any dead, damaged or unwanted growth over winter. Keep well watered until established.

Arbutus unedo: Killarney strawberry tree

Slow growing, and forming in time a gnarled trunk, this small evergreen tree makes a handsome specimen. Clusters of white flowers and red fruits are borne simultaneously in autumn, the fruit resembling strawberries in both colour and shape. Easy to maintain and elegant in appearance, this tree is a splendid addition to any garden setting.

Height × spread: 5 × 5m/16 ×16ft

Soil: Best grown in fertile, moist, neutral to acidic soil.

Position: Well suited to a position in sun or partial shade. Either grow as a specimen or place within a mixed or shrub border.

Care: No regular pruning required although hard pruning in spring will encourage regeneration. Keep well watered until established.

○ ◑ | ◌ | E | LH | ✹✹✹

Argyranthemum 'Vancouver': Marguerite

A pink, double flowered form of this frost tender sub-shrub whose daisy-type flowers are carried in profusion throughout the summer. Continuous dead heading will ensure an abundance of new flowers. A versatile plant which may be used to cover up the dying foliage of earlier flowering perennials in the herbaceous border.

Height × spread: 1 × 1m/3 × 3ft

Soil: Best grown in fertile, moist but well drained soil.

Position: Enjoys a hot, sunny position but will tolerate some shade.

Care: Not winter hardy. Either dig up the entire plant, transfer to a pot and overwinter in a frost free glasshouse or, alternatively, propagate from cuttings taken in late summer. Cuttings must be kept free from frost.

   ❄

Artemisia 'Powis Castle'

A fine evergreen shrub renowned for its ferny, silvery leaves which make an excellent foil to pale pinks, blues and rich purples in the mixed border. Cuttings taken in late summer root easily and will provide an insurance against loss in a severe winter. Older plants should be replaced periodically as they become woody.

Height × spread: 1 × 1.2m/3 × 4ft

Soil: Best grown in fertile, moist but well drained soil.

Position: Well suited to a position in full sun. Either grow as a specimen or place within a mixed or shrub border.

Care: Prune hard in late spring to encourage new growth, to retain the shape and to prevent woodiness. Keep well watered until established.

Berberis thunbergii **'Rose Glow'**: Barberry

An adaptable and versatile shrub which is cultivated mainly for its striking, variegated foliage which unfolds in the spring red-purple and, as the year progresses, matures with flecks of white. Small, shiny red berries in autumn follow the somewhat insignificant flowers of spring. Well suited to the smaller garden on account of its moderate size.

Height × spread: 1.2 × 1.2m/4 × 4ft

Soil: Best grown in fertile, moist but well drained soil.

Position: Well suited to a position in sun or partial shade. Either grow as a specimen or place within a mixed or shrub border.

Care: No regular pruning required. Remove any dead, damaged or unwanted growth over winter. Keep well watered until established.

◯ ◑ | ◊ | ❄❄❄

Betula utilis var. *jacquemontii*: Himalayan birch

For sheer whiteness of bark, then this birch has few rivals. A medium sized tree which is valued not only for its distinctive bark but also for its attractive autumn colour when leaves of mid-green turn to a warm golden-yellow before falling. A shallow root system restricts underplanting. Where space permits, plant as a group.

Height × spread: 18 × 10m/60 × 33ft

Soil: Best grown in fertile, moist but well drained soil. Generally unsuitable for chalk.

Position: Well suited to a position in sun or partial shade. Either grow as a specimen or place as a group within a woodland setting.

Care: No regular pruning required. Remove any dead, damaged or unwanted growth over winter. Keep well watered until established.

○ ◐ | ◊ | ❋❋❋

Buddleja alternifolia: Butterfly bush

Tight bunches of lilac flowers are produced in early summer along the entire length of the branches of this gracefully arching shrub. Sweetly scented, it is very attractive to butterflies, hence its common name of butterfly bush. It grows rapidly and regular thinning of old wood helps to retain an elegant shape. Excellent in the herbaceous border where a cascade of pastel colour is required.

Height × spread: 4 × 4m/13 × 13ft

Soil: Best grown in fertile, moist but well drained soil.

Position: Well suited to a position in sun. Either grow as a specimen or place within a mixed or shrub border.

Care: No regular pruning required. Remove any dead, damaged or unwanted growth over winter. Keep well watered until established.

| ○ | ○ | ✳✳✳ |

Buddleja crispa: Butterfly bush

One of the loveliest of all buddlejas, this shrub has luminous grey-green, felted leaves and the palest of lilac flowers in late summer. Its elegant, arching habit makes a dramatic display in the mixed border where it harmonizes well with a wide range of pastel coloured perennials. Not totally hardy, it is best given a warm, protected situation.

Height × spread: 2.4 × 2.4m/8 × 8ft

Soil: Best grown in fertile, moist but well drained soil.

Position: Well suited to a position in full sun. Either grow as a specimen or place within a mixed or shrub border.

Care: No regular pruning required. Remove any dead, damaged or unwanted growth over winter. Keep well watered until established.

○ ◐ ❉❉

Bupleurum fruticosum: Shrubby hare's ear

One of the principal attractions of this fairly hardy, evergreen shrub is its slightly shiny leaves of a deep blue-green. Above these, carried on short, stiff stems, appear rounded umbels of small golden flowers from late summer well into autumn. Foliage provides a good backdrop to other plantings whilst the whole shrub is well suited to hosting a climber.

Height × spread: 2 × 2.4m/6 × 8ft

Soil: Best grown in fertile, moist but well drained soil.

Position: Well suited to a position in full sun. Either grow as a specimen or place within a mixed or shrub border.

Care: No regular pruning required. Remove old flower spikes and cut back as necessary to determine size in spring. Keep well watered until established.

○ ⬡ E ❄❄❄ (borderline)

Buxus sempervirens **'Suffruticosa'**: Dwarf box

An absolute must for every garden where a note of formality is required. This completely hardy, dwarf evergreen shrub is an excellent subject to be planted as a low hedge or to be used, if required, for miniature topiary. As an edging to borders, as a single specimen or grown in a pot, this shrub has few equals.

Height × spread: 30 × 30cm/1 × 1ft in time

Soil: Best grown in fertile, moist but well drained soil. Benefits from feeding with compost or similar in the growing season.

Position: Well suited to a position in sun or partial shade. Either grow as a low hedge or use to form patterns.

Care: No regular pruning required. As an edging, clip to shape in late summer. Keep well watered until established.

| ○ ◑ | ◌ | E | ✳✳✳ |

Callicarpa bodinieri var. *giraldii*: Beauty berry

Grown not so much for the tiny pink flowers which
appear in summer, the principal delight of this deciduous
shrub is the mass of violet-purple, glistening berries which
follow and generously deck the branches in autumn, some
remaining until well after the fall of the leaves. An easy,
hardy shrub which deserves to be more widely grown.

Height × spread: 3 × 2.4m / 10 × 8ft

Soil: Best grown in fertile, moist but well drained soil.

Position: Well suited to a position in sun or partial shade. Either grow
as a specimen or place within a mixed or shrub border.

Care: No regular pruning required. Remove any dead, damaged or
unwanted growth over winter. Keep well watered until established.

Camellia japonica 'Nobilissima'

One of the delights of early spring, this hardy, evergreen shrub carries anemone-form, white flowers (with yellow shading as they fade) over dark green, glossy leaves at the start of the season. An excellent subject to include in a lightly wooded area out of the reach of cold, damaging winds. Camellias are available in a wide range of flower colour.

Height × spread: 3 × 2m/10 × 6ft

Soil: Best grown in fertile, moist, neutral to acidic soil.

Position: Well suited to a position in partial shade. Site away from the morning sun. Either grow as a specimen or place within a mixed or shrub border.

Care: No regular pruning required. Remove any dead, damaged or unwanted growth over winter. Keep well watered until established.

◑ ◔ E LH ❄❄❄

Caryopteris × *clandonensis*: Blue spiraea

A compact, sun-loving shrub of value on account of its attractive blue flowers produced in late summer and autumn. Borne on felty, aromatic, soft green leaves, bunches of tiny, lavender-blue flowers are carried in every axil of the long, arching stems. Several named forms are available including *C.* × *clandonensis* 'Worcester Gold', a recent introduction with golden foliage.

Height × spread: 75 × 75cm/2¹/₂ × 2¹/₂ft

Soil: Best grown in fertile, moist but well drained soil.

Position: Well suited to a position in sun or partial shade. Either grow as a specimen or place within a mixed or shrub border.

Care: As it flowers on the current season's growth, prune hard back to new shoots in spring. Keep well watered until established.

◑◐ ◊ ❄❄❄

This hardy, deciduous shrub of somewhat lax habit carries large panicles of pale, violet-blue flowers from midsummer into autumn over leaves of dark green. Effective when placed at the rear of an herbaceous border, particularly one where there is a concentration of late flowering perennials. Look out for a pink ceanothus, *C.* × *pallidus* 'Marie Simon'.

Height × spread: 1.5 × 1.5m/5 × 5ft

Soil: Best grown in fertile, moist but well drained soil. Chlorotic on shallow chalk.

Position: Well suited to a position in sun or partial shade. Either grow as a specimen or place within a mixed or shrub border.

Care: As it flowers on the current season's growth, prune hard back to new shoots in spring. Keep well watered until established.

◯ ◑ | ◊ | E | ❄❄❄

Because of its creeping habit, this low growing, hardy, evergreen shrub in time forms an effective ground cover. In spring flowers of an intense blue are carried over leaves of a shiny mid-green. Use as a host plant for a later flowering clematis to prolong the period of interest.

Height × spread: 1 × 2.4m/3 × 8ft

Soil: Best grown in fertile, moist but well drained soil.

Position: Well suited to a position in sun or partial shade. Either grow as a specimen or place within a mixed or shrub border.

Care: No regular pruning required. Remove any dead, damaged or unwanted growth over winter. Keep well watered until established.

◯ ◑ | ◌ | E | ❄❄❄

Cercis siliquastrum: Judas tree

In spring, when bare branches are covered in a mass of deep pink, pea-like flowers, this medium sized, deciduous tree is a most appealing sight. Later, heart-shaped leaves of blue-green develop which then turn yellow in the autumn. Where only a single tree can be accommodated, this is a good choice.

Height × spread: 10 × 10m/33 × 33ft

Soil: Best grown in fertile, moist but well drained soil.

Position: Well suited to a position in sun or partial shade. Either grow as a specimen or place within a mixed or shrub border.

Care: No regular pruning required. Remove any dead, damaged or unwanted growth over winter. Keep well watered until established.

◐ ◑ | ◊ | ✻✻✻

Chaenomeles × *superba* **'Pink Lady'**: Japonica

A lovely and very desirable shrub on account of its early spring flowers. 'Pink Lady' is of spreading habit. The spiny branches carry attractive pink-red flowers at the start of the year when they are welcome after the dark days of winter. Shiny leaves are of mid-green. Green fruits in autumn ripen to yellow.

Height × spread: 1.5 × 2m/5 × 6ft

Soil: Best grown in fertile, moist but well drained soil.

Position: Well suited to a position in full sun but tolerant of partial shade. Either grow as a specimen or place within a mixed or shrub border.

Care: No regular pruning required. Thin out old and crowded branches after flowering. Keep well watered until established.

○ ◑ | △ | ❄❄❄

Chimonanthus praecox: Wintersweet

This winter flowering, deciduous shrub is valued for its sweetly scented, waxy, lemon-cream flowers produced on bare stems before the emergence of new leaves. Suitable for training against a wall, it requires protection from cold winds in order to flower well. A charming and graceful shrub which is a stylish addition to the mixed border.

Height × spread: 4 × 3m/13 × 10ft

Soil: Best grown in fertile, moist but well drained soil.

Position: Well suited to a position in full sun. Either grow as a specimen or place within a mixed or shrub border.

Care: No regular pruning required. Thin out old and crowded branches after flowering. Keep well watered until established.

◯ ◊ ❋❋❋

Choisya ternata: Mexican orange blossom

The glossy, dark green, evergreen leaves of this deservedly popular shrub are topped in the late spring with pure white, starry flowers. Repeat flowering in late summer and autumn makes this an essential choice for the mixed border. An additional bonus is the strong scent of the flowers, making it attractive to both bees and butterflies.

Height × spread: 2.4 × 2.4m/8 × 8ft

Soil: Best grown in fertile, moist but well drained soil.

Position: Well suited to a position in full sun. Either grow as a specimen or place within a mixed or shrub border.

Care: No regular pruning required. Remove any dead, damaged or unwanted growth over winter. Keep well watered until established.

| ○ | ◌ | E | ❄❄❄ |

Cistus **'Elma'**: Rock rose, Sun rose

A frost-hardy, spreading shrub with evergreen, shiny, dark green leaves and pure white flowers with prominent yellow stamens in early summer. The delicate, papery flowers are produced in profusion when growing in favourable conditions. Full sun and protection from cold winds are a must for this shrub to do well.

Height × spread: 2 × 2m/6 × 6ft

Soil: Best grown in fairly fertile to poor, well drained soil. Intolerant of heavy chalk.

Position: Well suited to a position in full sun. Either grow as a specimen or place within a mixed or shrub border.

Care: No regular pruning required. Remove any dead, damaged or unwanted growth in spring. Plant in spring after danger of frost.

○ ◊ E ❄❄

Cistus × *purpureus*: Rock rose, Sun rose

Large, showy magenta-pink flowers, blotched with maroon, make a remarkable sight on this small, frost hardy, evergreen shrub in early summer. Suitable for a small garden, it enjoys a hot, sunny position and will tolerate drought conditions well. Sited at the front of a border or in the rock garden, it cannot fail to please.

Height × spread: 1 × 1m/3 × 3ft

Soil: Best grown in fairly fertile to poor, well drained soil.

Position: Well suited to a position in full sun. Either grow as a specimen or place within a mixed or shrub border.

Care: No regular pruning required. Remove any dead, damaged or unwanted growth in spring. Plant in spring after risk of frost.

○ ◊ E ❄❄

Clematis × *durandii*

Chosen for its striking, dark indigo-blue flowers, this non-clinging, frost-hardy climber is well worthy of consideration when selecting clematis. In midsummer the large, bold, unusual flowers can be allowed to trail through the border or trained vertically to provide a dramatic contrast to other flowering shrubs and perennials. Well worth seeking out.

Height × spread: Climbing or trailing to 2m/6ft.

Soil: Best grown in fertile, moist but well drained soil.

Position: Well suited to a position in full sun. Either train to cover a support or allow to scramble through a border.

Care: Cut down current season's growth completely to ground level after flowering or in the early spring. Keep well watered until established.

Clematis 'Gravetye Beauty'

The tulip-shaped flowers of this sophisticated, late
flowering clematis are a splendid crimson-red. Held erect
above dark green foliage, the flowers are produced in late
summer and continue right through until autumn.
Valuable for its end of season display, it may easily be
positioned to grow through earlier flowering shrubs.
Available most often from specialist nurseries.

Height × spread: Climbing or trailing to 2m/6ft.

Soil: Best grown in fertile, moist but well drained soil.

Position: Well suited to a position in full sun. Either train to cover a
support or allow to scramble through a border.

Care: Cut down current season's growth completely to ground level after
flowering or in the early spring. Keep well watered until established.

Clematis 'Mary Rose'

Massed heads of deep, dusky purple, fully double flowers, are carried from late summer until early autumn above a fine structure of pretty cut leaves and wiry stems. Vigorous in growth, this clematis will trail or climb extensively through the border or into shrubs where it will delight with its show at the close of the gardening year.

Height × spread: Climbing or trailing to 2m/6ft.

Soil: Best grown in fertile, moist but well drained soil.

Position: Well suited to a position in full sun. Either train to cover a support or allow to scramble through a border.

Care: Cut down current season's growth completely to ground level after flowering or in the early spring. Keep well watered until established.

○ ◐ ❋❋❋

Clematis 'Wada's Primrose'

A hybrid clematis flowering in mid-spring. Large, showy flowers, the sepals tapering to a point, are of pale cream with a deeper, central stripe. Altogether a very handsome and appealing climber, though in full sun, the flowers will fade. Like all clematis, especially the large-flowered hybrids, the root ball needs planting 7.5cm/3in below the earth surface, as a precaution against wilt.

Height × spread: Climbing or trailing to 2m/6ft.

Soil: For any well drained moist soil.

Position: Suitable for planting against a wall but equally effective when allowed to trail through a border or to reach into the lower branches of a shrub or tree. Best in full sun or part shade.

Care: Light prune in early spring when any dead wood should be removed. Enrich annually with garden compost or well rotted manure.

Cordyline australis 'Purpurea': Cabbage palm

Guaranteed to give an exotic feel to any area in which it is planted, this frost hardy, evergreen shrub has a palm-like habit. The sword-like leaves have a bronze-purple glow and give dramatic contrast of colour and form to other pale leafed shrubs and perennials. Suitable for growing in a container when it can be moved around for immediate effect.

Height × spread: 3 × 1m/10 × 3ft

Soil: Best grown in fertile, moist but well drained soil.

Position: Well suited to a position in sun or partial shade. Either grow as a specimen or place within a mixed or shrub border.

Care: No regular pruning required. Remove any dead, damaged or unwanted growth in spring. Keep well protected in winter.

○ ◑ | ◇ | E | ❄❄

Cornus canadensis: Creeping dogwood

The quiet charm of this ground hugging, deciduous plant lies in the pretty contrast of the starry, white-green flowers with the glossy mid-green leaves of its foliage. Flowering in late spring to early summer, this is followed by red fruits in autumn. An acid lover, its growth is more vigorous given those conditions.

Height × spread: 15cm/6in × indefinite spread

Soil: Best grown in fertile, moist but well drained acidic to neutral soil.

Position: Well suited to a position in sun or partial shade. Allow to creep as a form of ground cover at the base of shrubs and trees.

Care: Cut down current season's growth to ground level at the year's end. Keep well watered until established.

○ ◑ | ◊ | LH | ✳✳✳

Cornus florida f. *rubra*: Dogwood

The very slow growing habit of this deciduous tree makes it a suitable choice for a small garden. Showy pink bracts are produced in spring and the mid-green leaves colour to a rich red-purple in autumn. Best situated in a sheltered position out of the reach of cold winds which are likely to result in leaf scorch.

Height × spread: 6 × 7.5m/20 × 25ft

Soil: Best grown in fertile, moist but well drained, neutral to acid soil.

Position: Well suited to a position in sun or partial shade. Either grow as a specimen or place within a mixed or shrub border.

Care: No regular pruning required. Remove any dead, damaged or unwanted growth over winter. Keep well watered until established.

○ ◐ | ◊ | LH | ✻✻✻

Cornus kousa var. *chinensis*: Dogwood

Possibly the most glamorous and dramatic of all the dogwoods, this shrub has distinctive creamy-white flower bracts, maturing to pinky-red, in summer. Autumn colour of crimson-red foliage is accompanied by unusual, red, strawberry-like fruits. A most elegant and stylish addition to the garden and one which will always elicit favourable comment.

Height × spread: 7 × 5m/23 × 16ft

Soil: Best grown in fertile, moist but well drained soil.

Position: Well suited to a position in sun or partial shade. Either grow as a specimen or place within a mixed or shrub border.

Care: No regular pruning required. Remove any dead, damaged or unwanted growth over winter. Keep well watered until established.

Corylopsis pauciflora

Pale lemon, highly scented flowers hang in clusters on bare stems in spring on this dense and bushy shrub of upright but spreading habit. When it emerges the foliage is flushed with bronze but later it develops into a bright green. A lover of acid soil, it will not thrive where lime is present. Afford some protection from cold winds to encourage flowers.

Height × spread: 1.5 × 2.5m/5 × 8ft

Soil: Best grown in fertile, moist but well drained acidic soil.

Position: Well suited to a position in full sun but tolerant of partial shade. Either grow as a specimen or place within a mixed or shrub border.

Care: No regular pruning required. Thin out old and crowded branches after flowering. Keep well watered until established.

○ ◑ | ◐ | LH | ✿✿✿

Cotinus coggygria **'Royal Purple'**: Smoke bush

Eventually becoming large and spreading, this shrub is of great value for its dark, plummy foliage which contrasts well with a wide range of other shrubs and perennials. Smoky plume-like flowerheads are produced in profusion in summer whilst in autumn the foliage turns a rich vibrant scarlet. Use this shrub to act as a host to a clematis or other climber.

Height × spread: 5 × 5m/16 × 16ft

Soil: Best grown in fertile, moist but well drained soil.

Position: Well suited to a position in sun or partial shade. Either grow as a specimen or place within a mixed or shrub border.

Care: No regular pruning required. Remove any dead, damaged or unwanted growth over winter. Keep well watered until established.

○ ◑ | ◊ | ✳✳✳

Pale cream flowers appear to pour over the arching stems of this low growing, deciduous shrub in late spring. The delicately scented, pea-like flowers are produced in abundance seeming to cover the entire shrub. An excellent, small shrub for providing an early splash of colour and well suited for inclusion where garden space is restricted.

Height × spread: 30cm × 1.5m/1 × 5ft

Soil: Best grown in fertile, moist but well drained soil.

Position: Well suited to a position in full sun. Either grow as a specimen or place within a mixed or shrub border.

Care: Immediately after flowering, shorten the previous year's growth by half. Avoid pruning old wood. Keep well watered until established.

| ◑ | ◊ | ❄❄❄ |

Daphne bholua

Queen of shrubs, the daphne is certainly a superior addition to any mixed border. This species is a deciduous or evergreen shrub of upright habit with slender, shiny leaves of dark green. The clusters of white, pink tinged flowers are heavily scented and are produced in abundance in the late winter. The flowers are followed by dramatic, purple-black fruits.

Height × spread: 2 × 1m/6 × 3ft

Soil: Best grown in fertile, moist but well drained soil. Prefers neutral to alkaline conditions.

Position: Well suited to a position in sun or partial shade. Either grow as a specimen or place within a mixed or shrub border.

Care: No regular pruning required. Remove any dead, damaged or unwanted growth over winter. Keep well watered until established.

Daphne mezereum

Clusters of purple-pink, heavily scented flowers are produced on bare woody stems in late winter and early spring. Pale green, lance-shaped leaves follow to clothe the branches of this deciduous shrub and are accompanied by the formation later of bright red fruits. No winter border should be without this regal performer.

Height × spread: 1.2 × 1m/4 × 3ft

Soil: Best grown in fertile, moist but well drained soil. Prefers neutral to alkaline conditions.

Position: Well suited to a position in sun or partial shade. Either grow as a specimen or place within a mixed or shrub border.

Care: No regular pruning required. Remove any dead, damaged or unwanted growth over winter. Keep well watered until established.

○ ◑ | ◊ | ❋❋❋

Daphne odora

The heavenly scent of this majestic, frost hardy, evergreen shrub is without equal. Shiny, dark green leaves carry clusters of fragrant, pale lilac-pink flowers from late winter to early spring followed by red fruits. Capable of filling an entire garden with perfume, this shrub is an aristocrat of the winter border. There is also a form with yellow-margined leaves called *D. o.* 'Aureomarginata'.

Height × spread: 1.5 × 1.5m/5 × 5ft

Soil: Best grown in fertile, moist but well drained soil. Prefers neutral to alkaline conditions.

Position: Well suited to a position in sun or partial shade. Either grow as a specimen or place within a mixed or shrub border.

Care: No regular pruning required. Remove any dead, damaged or unwanted growth over winter. Keep well watered until established.

Davidia involucrata: Handkerchief tree

Grown for its remarkable hanging white bracts, this deciduous tree with mid-green leaves creates a ghostly appearance when in full flower in late spring. Indeed, it is sometimes named the ghost tree. Slow to attain its full height, it is surprisingly sensitive to cold winds and frosts when young. It is best, therefore, to site it in a sheltered, warm position.

Height × spread: 15 × 10m/49 × 33ft

Soil: Best grown in fertile, moist but well drained soil.

Position: Well suited to a position in sun or partial shade. Either grow as a specimen or place within a mixed or shrub border.

Care: No regular pruning required. Remove any dead, damaged or unwanted growth over winter. Keep well watered until established.

○ ◑ | △ | ❄ ❄ ❄

Drimys lanceolata

A handsome, frost-hardy, evergreen shrub, not generally widely grown, with glossy, aromatic leaves and clusters of small, white, starry flowers in spring. Appreciative of a warm, sheltered position in the garden, it will reward with abundant flowering. Another form, *D. winteri*, is also valuable as a small tree with aromatic bark and scented flowers.

Height × spread: 4 × 2.4m/13 × 8ft

Soil: Best grown in fertile, moist but well drained soil.

Position: Well suited to a position in sun or partial shade. Either grow as a specimen or place within a mixed or shrub border.

Care: No regular pruning required. Remove any dead, damaged or unwanted growth over winter. Keep well watered until established.

○ ◑ | ◊ | E | ❄❄

Embothrium coccineum: Chilean fire bush

Truly spectacular when in full flower, this frost hardy, suckering tree is worth planting in every garden where there is space to show it off to advantage. Dense racemes of showy, bottlebrush type flowerheads of brilliant scarlet-orange are produced on long, wand-like branches in late spring and early summer. Semi-evergreen in extremes of cold.

Height × spread: 10 × 5m/33 × 16ft

Soil: Best grown in fertile, moist but well drained neutral to acidic soil.

Position: Well suited to a position in sun or partial shade. Either grow as a specimen or place within a mixed or shrub border.

Care: Minimal pruning required. Remove any dead, damaged or unwanted growth over winter. Keep well watered until established.

○ ◑ | ◌ | E/Semi-E | LH | ❋❋

Eucryphia × intermedia

A glory of the garden for its late flowering habit, this evergreen tree of upright growth provides a spectacular show in maturity. The shiny leaves of dark green present a perfect background to the cup-shaped, scented white flowers with golden stamens which are carried from late summer to autumn. Prefers a cool root run.

Height × spread: 10 × 6m/33 × 20ft

Soil: Best grown in fertile, moist but well drained neutral to acidic soil.

Position: Well suited to a position in full sun. Either grow as a specimen or place within a mixed or shrub border.

Care: No regular pruning required. Remove any dead, damaged or unwanted growth over winter. Keep well watered until established.

◯ ◗ E LH ❄❄❄ (borderline)

Euonymus planipes: Spindle tree

This small, upright deciduous shrub can often be
overlooked early in the season when its mid-green leaves
and inconspicuous flowers seem unremarkable. With the
onset of autumn, however, the whole shrub turns flame-
red and hanging fruits of glowing crimson are produced. It
is then that its true value can be fully appreciated.

Height × spread: 3 × 3m/10 × 10ft

Soil: Best grown in fertile, moist but well drained soil.

Position: Well suited to a position in sun or partial shade. Either grow
as a specimen or place within a mixed or shrub border.

Care: No regular pruning required. Remove any dead, damaged or
unwanted growth over winter. Keep well watered until established.

○ ◑ | ◊ | ✳✳✳

Exochorda × *macrantha* 'The Bride'

Sprays of thin, arching branches of this spreading deciduous shrub carry an abundance of open, cup-shaped, glistening white flowers in late spring and early summer. Attractive in habit and tolerant of a wide range of growing conditions, this is a reliably good performer for the mixed or shrub border, and makes a splendid showy specimen.

Height × spread: 2 × 3m/6 × 10ft

Soil: Best grown in fertile, moist but well drained soil. Tolerant of chalk.

Position: Well suited to a position in sun or partial shade. Either grow as a specimen or place within a mixed or shrub border.

Care: No regular pruning required. Thin out old and crowded branches after flowering. Keep well watered until established.

○ ◑ | ◌ | ❄❄❄

Fagus sylvatica: Beech

Clipped to shape annually, this otherwise large tree will form an excellent hedge which will retain its foliage over winter. New leaves emerge fresh green at the start of the season and remain so until the approach of autumn when they colour, albeit fleetingly, a wonderful yellow and orange-brown. This winter cover makes it one of the best deciduous hedges.

Height × spread: 25 × 15m/82 × 49ft as a tree.

Soil: Best grown in fertile, moist but well drained soil. Tolerant of chalk.

Position: Well suited to a positon in sun or partial shade. Either grow as a specimen tree or plant as a hedge.

Care: No regular pruning required. As a hedge, clip to shape in late summer. Keep well watered until established.

○ ◑ | ◊ | ❊❊❊

Fothergilla major

A slow growing, deciduous shrub which is valued for its scented, white bottlebrush-type flowers produced in late spring and early summer as well as for its remarkable late season colour. In autumn the dark green leaves turn all shades of flame giving the whole shrub a bonfire-like appearance of amazing intensity.

Height × spread: 2.4 × 2m/8 × 6ft

Soil: Best grown in humus-rich, moist but well drained acidic to neutral soil.

Position: Well suited to a position in sun or partial shade. Either grow as a specimen or place within a mixed or shrub border.

Care: No regular pruning required. Remove any dead, damaged or unwanted growth over winter. Keep well watered until established.

◯ ◑ | ◊ | LH | ❄❄❄

Fremontodendron mexicanum: Flannel bush

Enjoy this evergreen or semi-evergreen, frost hardy shrub of upright habit for its golden-yellow flowers which are produced against healthy, dark green foliage from late spring until autumn. Although it may be grown as a specimen shrub, it is probably best suited, certainly in colder areas, to being trained against a wall. Almost always certain to attract attention.

Height × spread: 6 × 4m/20 × 13ft

Soil: For well drained, fertile soil which does not dry out.

Position: Best grown against a warm, sheltered wall in full sun out of the reach of cold, damaging winds.

Care: No regular pruning. Thin out old wood after flowering. Remove winter damaged growth in spring.

| ○ | ◊ | E or Semi-E | ✳✳ |

Fuchsia 'Thalia'

This superior form of fuchsia is a frost tender shrub of upright habit. The dark foliage contrasts with, yet complements, the startling, flame coloured tubular flowers which are produced in late summer. A most elegant choice for summer bedding. It is one of the most popular cultivars of the Triphylla Group of fuchsias.

Height × spread: 60 × 60cm/2 × 2ft

Soil: Best grown in fertile, moist but well drained soil.

Position: Well suited to a position in full sun. Place as required in the herbaceous or mixed border or appropriate garden situation.

Care: Not winter hardy. In cold areas propagate from cuttings in late summer and overwinter in a frost-free glasshouse. Alternatively, dig up, pot and protect from frost.

Garrya elliptica

An evergreen, frost hardy shrub whose shiny grey-green foliage is beautifully offset by clusters of long, woolly, hanging catkins of a lustrous blue-grey from mid-winter to early spring. Given a sheltered position, such as a warm wall, then *G. elliptica* generally proves to be hardy. Include as an unusual backdrop to a mixed border.

Height × spread: 4 × 4m/13 × 13ft

Soil: Best grown in fertile, moist but well drained soil.

Position: Well suited to a position in full sun or part shade. Either grow as a specimen or place within a mixed or shrub border.

Care: No regular pruning required. Remove any dead, damaged or unwanted growth over winter. Keep well watered until established.

Halesia monticola: Snowdrop tree

Surprisingly seldom seen, this deciduous tree is charming when in flower in late spring. Hanging bells of white flowers are produced with fresh green leaves and are followed later in the season by green, winged fruit. A final flourish to complete the gardening year is achieved in autumn when leaves turn butter-yellow.

Height × spread: 12 × 7.5m/39 × 25ft

Soil: Best grown in humus-rich, moisture retentive acidic to neutral soil.

Position: Well suited to a position in sun or partial shade. Either grow as a specimen or place within a mixed or shrub border.

Care: No regular pruning required. Remove any dead, damaged or unwanted growth over winter. Keep well watered until established.

◐ ◑ | ◉ | LH | ✳✳✳

× *Halimiocistus sahucii*

If space is at a premium, then this small, evergreen, mound-forming shrub cannot fail to please. Open, saucer-shaped pure white flowers with butter-yellow centres are carried in abundance in summer over dark green leaves. Enjoying the sun and tolerant of drought conditions, this shrub is perfect for the gravel, rock or Mediterranean gardens.

Height × spread: 45cm × 1m/1½ × 3ft

Soil: Best grown in fairly fertile to poor, light, well drained soil.

Position: Well suited to a position in full sun. Either grow as a specimen or place within a mixed or shrub border.

Care: No regular pruning required. Remove any dead, damaged or unwanted growth over winter. Keep well watered until established.

Hamamelis × intermedia 'Pallida': Witch hazel

The witch hazels remain supreme for their winter colour provided during one of the bleakest of times in the gardening year. This variety is an upright, deciduous shrub producing spidery, scented flowerheads of pale lemon-yellow in late winter on bare, woody branches. The mid-green oval leaves turn to good autumn shades of yellow that complete the end of season display.

Height × spread: 4 × 4m/13 × 13ft

Soil: Best grown in humus-rich, moist but well drained acidic to neutral soil.

Position: Well suited to a position in sun or partial shade. Either grow as a specimen or place within a mixed or shrub border.

Care: No regular pruning required. Remove any dead, damaged or unwanted growth over winter. Keep well watered until established.

◐ ◑ ◌ LH ❄❄❄

Hebe 'Pewter Dome'

A frost hardy, evergreen, dome-shaped shrub of compact
habit. The pale grey-green leaves carry racemes of small,
snow white flowers in late spring and early summer. An
ideal shrub with which to break up the flow of a border to
create a definite, and deliberate, point of interest. *H.
cupressoides* 'Boughton Dome', though smaller and
generally non-flowering, forms a dome also. It has dark
green foliage.

Height × spread: 1 × 1m/3 × 3ft

Soil: Best grown in fertile, moist but well drained soil.

Position: Well suited to a position in sun or partial shade. Either grow
as a specimen or place within a mixed or shrub border.

Care: No regular pruning required. Remove any dead, damaged or
unwanted growth after flowering. Keep well watered until established.

◐ ◑ | ◊ | E | ❄❄

Hibiscus syriacus 'Blue Bird'

An eye-catching, deciduous shrub of upright habit with flowers of a remarkable violet-blue in late summer. The lobed and toothed leaves of dark green deepen the intensity of the flowers to give a truly spectacular show in the late season border. Other varieties are available with flowers ranging in colour from blue, pink, purple, red and white to yellow.

Height × spread: 2 × 2m/6 × 6ft

Soil: Best grown in fertile, moist but well drained soil.

Position: Well suited to a position in full sun. Either grow as a specimen or place within a mixed or shrub border.

Care: No regular pruning required. Remove any dead, damaged or unwanted growth over winter. Keep well watered until established.

◑ ◊ ❋❋❋

Hydrangea arborescens **'Annabelle'**: Sevenbark

An unusual form of a well known and frequently
employed shrub. Dark green, heart-shaped leaves set off
dull white flowers in summer which gradually age to pale
then deeper shades of green. Very free flowering, the
flowerheads last well into autumn and may, if desired, be
dried. Inclined to be of suckering habit.

Height × spread: 2.4 × 2.4m/8 × 8ft

Soil: Best grown in fertile, moisture retentive soil which is not allowed
to dry out.

Position: Well suited to a position in sun or partial shade. Either grow
as a specimen or place within a mixed or shrub border.

Care: No regular pruning required. Remove any dead, damaged or
unwanted growth over winter. Keep well watered until established.

○ ◑ ◐ | ☀ ❊❊❊

Hydrangea aspera

Large dark blue-green leaves form the perfect backdrop to the highly attractive, lace-cap flowerheads of faded lilac-blue formed in late summer. Slowly growing to a large, deciduous shrub, it is an impressive sight when fully grown, the old wood taking on a gnarled appearance. Underplant with *Hosta lancifolia* with its violet-blue flowers.

Height × spread: 2.4 × 2m/8 × 6ft

Soil: Best grown in humus-rich, moisture retentive soil, which does not dry out.

Position: Well suited to a position in partial shade. Either grow as a specimen or place within a mixed or shrub border.

Care: No regular pruning required. Remove any dead, damaged or unwanted growth over winter. Keep well watered until established.

◑ ◔ ❄❄❄

Hydrangea quercifolia: Oak-leafed hydrangea

As its common name suggests, the oak-like leaves of this hydrangea make it definitely different from other species. The mid-green leaves turn a wonderful purple, the colour of ripened grapes, towards autumn. In addition, lacy panicles of light cream flowers, becoming tinged pink with age, are produced from midsummer to autumn.

Height × spread: 1.5 × 2m/5 × 6ft

Soil: Best grown in fertile, moisture retentive soil which is not allowed to dry out.

Position: Well suited to a position in sun or partial shade. Either grow as a specimen or place within a mixed or shrub border.

Care: No regular pruning required. Remove any dead, damaged or unwanted growth over winter. Keep well watered until established.

○ ◑ | ◐ | ❄❄❄

Ilex aquifolium 'Ferox Argentea': Silver hedgehog holly

An unusual feature of this evergreen holly is the way in which the variegated leaves of mid-green, margined with cream, carry surface spines, making for an exceedingly prickly bush. Young branches are, when new, flushed with purple. Use to add a touch of colour to an otherwise dull or uninteresting area of the garden, particularly in winter.

Height × spread: 6 × 4m/20 × 13ft

Soil: Best grown in fertile, moist but well drained soil.

Position: Well suited to a position in sun or partial shade. Either grow as a specimen or place within a mixed or shrub border.

Care: No regular pruning required. Remove any dead, damaged or unwanted growth over winter. Keep well watered until established.

◖ ◕ | ◌ | E | ❋❋❋

Indigofera heterantha

Magenta-pink, pea-like flowers are produced on sparsely leafed stems in early summer followed by a delicate tracery of finely cut, fresh green foliage. The freely branching habit of this deciduous shrub gives it an elegant and attractive appearance which combines easily with a wide range of shrubs and perennials in a mixed border.

Height × spread: 2 × 2m/6 × 6ft

Soil: Best grown in fertile, moist but well drained soil. Tolerant of dry conditions.

Position: Well suited to a position in full sun. Either grow as a specimen or place within a mixed or shrub border.

Care: Pruning may either be restricted to the removal of any dead or damaged wood or all stems may be cut to ground level in spring.

Itea ilicifolia

A frost hardy, evergreen shrub with holly-like leaves and producing long, ice-green, scented catkin inflorescences in summer. Enjoying a sunny situation, its flowers are encouraged when branches are trained against a warm wall. Unusual and showy, *I. ilicifolia* is an excellent, out-of-the-ordinary choice for any garden and, on account of its moderate size, is not difficult to place if it can be given shelter.

Height × spread: 3 × 3m/10 × 10ft

Soil: Best grown in fertile, moist but well drained soil.

Position: Well suited to a position in full sun. Either grow as a specimen, on a wall for shelter or place within a mixed or shrub border.

Care: No regular pruning required. Remove any dead, damaged or unwanted growth over winter. Keep well watered until established.

Kalmia latifolia: Calico bush

Given acidic conditions, then this is a delightful, slow growing evergreen shrub to include in the garden where it will reward with an extraordinary profusion of sugar-pink, deep pink or red flowerheads almost entirely covering the shiny, dark-green foliage from late spring to midsummer. The slightest suggestion of chalk, however, will result in failure to thrive and, most likely, death.

Height × spread: 3 × 3m/10 × 10ft

Soil: Best grown in humus-rich, moist but well drained acidic to neutral soil.

Position: Well suited to a position in sun or partial shade. Either grow as a specimen or place within a mixed or shrub border.

Care: No regular pruning required. Remove any dead, damaged or unwanted growth over winter. Keep well watered until established.

○ ◑ | ◗ | E | LH | ❋❋❋

Koelreuteria paniculata: Pride of India

An elegant tree of domed habit which benefits from a position in full sun not only to grow well, but also to highlight the panicles of golden-yellow flowers which are produced in mid to late summer, followed by fruit capsules. Pinnate leaves of dark green open red in late spring, turning to a wonderful butter-yellow in autumn.

Height × **spread:** 10 × 10m/33 × 33ft

Soil: Best grown in fertile, moist but well drained soil.

Position: Well suited to a position in full sun. Either grow as a specimen or place within a mixed or shrub border.

Care: No regular pruning required. Remove any dead, damaged or unwanted growth over winter. Keep well watered until established.

| ◯ | ◊ | ❋❋❋ |

Kolkwitzia amabilis: Beauty bush

Prolific in its flowering habit, this deciduous shrub is one of the joys of the late spring and early summer border when it produces a mass of pale pink, foxglove-like flowers flushed with yellow. Long, arching stems carry dark green foliage which deepens to shades of red at the approach of autumn. The cultivar called 'Pink Cloud' has flowers of a rich pink.

Height × spread: 3 × 3m/10 × 10ft

Soil: Best grown in fertile, moist but well drained soil.

Position: Well suited to a position in full sun. Either grow as a specimen or place within a mixed or shrub border.

Care: No regular pruning required. Remove any dead, damaged or unwanted growth over winter. Keep well watered until established.

○ ◐ ✳✳✳

Lavandula stoechas: French lavender

Provided this species lavender is planted in a warm, sunny spot, then it should prove relatively hardy. A compact, evergreen shrub with leaves of grey-green and carrying striking scented flower spikes of deep purple from late spring to summer. Lovely when planted to edge a path. Both flowers and leaves may be dried and used for pot-pourri.

Height × spread: 60 × 60cm/2 × 2ft

Soil: Best grown in fertile, light, well drained soil.

Position: Well suited to a position in full sun. Either grow as a specimen or place within a mixed or shrub border.

Care: As it flowers on the current season's growth, prune hard back to new shoots in spring. Keep well watered until established.

◯ ◊ E ❄❄❄ (borderline)

Lavatera 'Burgundy Wine': Mallow

Shown here growing through a haze of the perennial
Verbena bonariensis, this hardy, semi-evergreen sub-shrub
carries lobed grey-green foliage and open flowers of, as its
name suggests, a rich wine-red all through the summer.
An easy plant in cultivation and one with a long flowering
season which associates well with many border
perennials.

Height × spread: 2 × 2m/6 × 6ft

Soil: Best grown in fertile, light and well drained soil.

Position: Well suited to a position in full sun. Either grow as a
specimen or place wtihin a mixed or shrub border.

Care: As it flowers on the current season's growth, prune hard back to
new shoots in spring. Keep well watered until established.

◐ | △ | Semi-E | ❄❄❄

A hardy, deciduous tree which is valued for its maple-like leaves which, in the autumn, turn from mid-green to a spectacular flame colour in shades of scarlet, crimson and purple-red. The young branches have a texture which closely resembles that of cork. It is ideally placed where its conical shape may be fully appreciated.

Height × spread: 25 × 12m/82 × 39ft

Soil: Best grown in fertile, moist, neutral to acidic soil.

Position: Well suited to a position in sun or partial shade. Either grow as a specimen or place within a woodland situation.

Care: No regular pruning required. Remove any dead, damaged or unwanted growth over winter. Keep well watered until established.

○ ◑ | ◊ | LH | ❋❋❋

Lupinus arboreus: Tree lupin

Although this frost hardy, semi-evergreen or evergreen shrub is not particularly long lived, it is most useful for filling a space in the border. In late spring and summer spikes of scented yellow flowers, occasionally blue, are carried over divided leaves of grey-green. Look out for seedlings, usually to be found close to the parent plant.

Height × spread: 2 × 2m/6 × 6ft

Soil: Best grown in fertile, moist but well drained soil.

Position: Well suited to a position in sun or partial shade. Either grow as a specimen or place within a mixed or shrub border.

Care: No regular pruning required. Remove any dead, damaged or unwanted growth in spring. Keep well watered until established.

○ ◑ | ◊ | E | ❄❄

Magnolia grandiflora 'Exmouth'

A lovely, hardy, evergreen tree to include in the garden
wherever there is sufficient space. Light green leaves are
brown felted on the undersides and set off large, scented,
cup-shaped flowers of cream from late summer to early
autumn. May be trained to grow against a wall where it
will enjoy both the warmth and shelter.

Height × **spread:** 10 × 10m/33 × 33ft

Soil: Best grown in fertile, moist, neutral to acidic soil.

Position: Well suited to a position in sun or partial shade. Either grow
as a specimen or place within a mixed or shrub border.

Care: No regular pruning required. Remove any dead, damaged or
unwanted growth over winter. Keep well watered until established.

| ☉ ◑ | ◊ | E | LH | ✳✳✳ |

Magnolia liliiflora 'Nigra'

Where space is perhaps restricted, then this hardy, deciduous shrub of compact habit is a good choice. Dark green leaves accompany upright, goblet-shaped flowers of a deep purple-red in early summer with a few blooms appearing occasionally in autumn. As with many magnolias, both flowers and foliage may be damaged by late frosts.

Height × spread: 3 × 2.4m / 10 × 8ft

Soil: Best grown in fertile, moist, neutral to acidic soil.

Position: Well suited to a position in sun or partial shade. Either grow as a specimen or place within a mixed or shrub border.

Care: No regular pruning required. Remove any dead, damaged or unwanted growth over winter. Keep well watered until established.

○ ◑ | ◊ | LH | ❊❊❊

Mahonia lomariifolia

In maturity this frost-hardy, evergreen shrub is bound to excite comment. Of upright habit, with pinnate leathery leaves of dark green, it carries racemes of scented yellow flowers from late autumn to winter, later to be followed by blue-black berries. Best in a position out of the reach of cold, damaging winds.

Height × spread: 3 × 2m / 10 × 6ft

Soil: Best grown in fertile, moist but well drained soil.

Position: Well suited to a position in full sun. Either grow as a specimen or place within a mixed or shrub border.

Care: No regular pruning required. Remove any dead, damaged or unwanted growth over winter. Keep well watered until established.

○	◊	E	✳✳

Malus hupehensis: Crab apple

An excellent choice of tree for any garden as its early blossom and end of year crab apples make for an extended period of interest. In spring a mature specimen is massed with tiny, scented white flowers to be followed later with an abundance of cherry-red fruits from which is derived the common name.

Height × spread: 12 × 12m/39 × 39ft

Soil: Best grown in fertile, moist but well drained soil.

Position: Well suited to a position in full sun. Either grow as a specimen or place within a mixed or shrub border.

Care: No regular pruning required. Remove any dead, damaged or unwanted growth over winter. Keep well watered until established.

○ ◊ ❅❅❅

Melianthus major: Honey bush

A half-hardy, evergreen shrub noted for its bold, lustrous foliage of finely cut, grey-green leaves which are produced from late spring to midsummer. Unlikely to flower (the flowers are a dark rusty red on tall stems in late spring to summer), it is best grown either as a specimen foliage plant in the border or in a large container. Eye-catching and exotic in appearance.

Height × spread: 2 × 1m/6 × 3ft

Soil: Best grown in fertile, moist but well drained soil.

Position: Well suited to a position in full sun. Either grow as a specimen or place within a mixed or shrub border.

Care: No regular pruning required. Remove any spent flowerheads and dead leaves to keep the plant looking good all year round. Protect from frost. Keep well watered until established.

Myrtus communis: Myrtle

It is a great pity that in colder areas this evergreen tree must be considered as only frost hardy. Of upright habit, it has aromatic leaves of a shiny, dark green over which are carried white flowers in summer and early autumn to be followed by deep purple, near black fruits. May be trained against a wall.

Height × spread: 3 × 3m/10 × 10ft

Soil: Best grown in fertile, moist but well drained soil.

Position: Well suited to a position in full sun. Either grow as a specimen or place within a mixed or shrub border.

Care: No regular pruning required. Remove any dead, damaged or unwanted growth in spring. Keep well watered until established.

○ ◇ E ❄❄

Neillia thibetica

This hardy, deciduous shrub deserves to be more widely
grown for it is easy in cultivation and can, on account of
its suckering habit, be employed as a form of screen.
Stems of red-brown carry bright green leaves and racemes
of tubular rose-pink flowers in early summer. It is at its
best in a slightly informal situation.

Height × spread: 2 × 2m/6 × 6ft

Soil: Best grown in fertile, moist but well drained soil.

Position: Well suited to a position in sun or partial shade. Either grow
as a specimen or place within a mixed or shrub border.

Care: No regular pruning required. Remove any dead, damaged or
unwanted growth over winter. Keep well watered until established.

Nyssa sylvatica: Black gum

A handsome tree which is largely cultivated for the brilliance of its autumn colour. It is worth growing for its attractive foliage, as the leaves of dark green turn to shades of red, orange and yellow before they finally fall. Wonderful when included in a scheme designed primarily for an end of season effect. Position away from cold winds. It is broadly conical in outline.

Height × spread: 20 × 10m/70 × 33ft

Soil: Best grown in fertile, moist, neutral to acidic soil.

Position: Well suited to a position in sun or partial shade. Either grow as a specimen or place within a woodland situation.

Care: No regular pruning required. Remove any dead, damaged or unwanted growth over winter. Keep well watered until established.

◐ ● | ◊ | LH | ❄❄❄

Osmanthus delavayi

An attractive, hardy, evergreen shrub of rounded habit with arching stems carrying leaves of dark green which, in spring, are smothered with highly scented, tubular white flowers, the fragrance of which will fill an entire garden on a still day. In turn these are followed by blue-black fruits. It is well suited to a wide range of situations.

Height × spread: 4 × 4m/13 × 13ft

Soil: Best grown in fertile, moist but well drained soil.

Position: Well suited to a position in sun or partial shade. Either grow as a specimen or place within a mixed or shrub border.

Care: No regular pruning required. Remove any dead, damaged or unwanted growth over winter. Keep well watered until established.

Paeonia delavayi var. *ludlowii*: Tree peony

This hardy, deciduous shrub is certainly worthy of a place in any garden. Accompanying foliage of bright, fresh green pointed leaflets are large, single flowers of clear yellow in late spring creating an impact wherever the plant is sited. For deep red flowers, then select *P. delavayi* which is similar although a little later.

Height × spread: 2 × 1.2m/6 × 4ft

Soil: Best grown in humus-rich, moist but well drained soil.

Position: Well suited to a position in sun or partial shade. Either grow as a specimen or place within a mixed or shrub border.

Care: No regular pruning required. Remove any dead, damaged or unwanted growth over winter. Keep well watered until established.

○ ◑ | ◊ | ✽✽✽

Perovskia atriplicifolia: Russian sage

This small, hardy, deciduous subshrub delays flowering until late summer and early autumn when its spires of tubular, violet-blue flowers are particularly appreciated. Additionally, aromatic foliage of grey-green is an excellent foil to other plantings. Wonderful when placed in a group of a few plants together to create a wash of blue.

Height × spread: 1.2 × 1m/4 × 3ft

Soil: Best grown in fertile, moist but well drained soil. Tolerant of chalk.

Position: Well suited to a position in full sun. Either grow as a specimen or place within a mixed or shrub border.

Care: As it flowers on the current season's growth, prune hard back to new shoots in spring. Keep well watered until established.

◐ ◊ ✳✳✳

Philadelphus **'Manteau d'Hermine'**: Mock orange

Where space is insufficient to accommodate one of the larger mock orange bushes, then this variety is an excellent alternative. A hardy, deciduous shrub, it is valued not only for its compact habit but also for its highly scented, creamy-white, very double flowers which are carried over light green leaves in early and midsummer. A good cultivar for the small garden.

Height × spread: 75cm × 1.5m/2.5 × 5ft

Soil: Best grown in fertile, moist but well drained soil.

Position: Well suited to a position in full sun. Either grow as a specimen or place within a mixed or shrub border.

Care: As it flowers on the current season's growth, prune hard back to new shoots in spring. Keep well watered until established.

| ○ | ◊ | ❋❋❋ |

Less well known than *P.* 'Belle Etoile', this mock orange is well deserving of a place in the garden. A hardy, deciduous shrub it carries single, scented white flowers, marked with purple at the centre, on arching stems in early and midsummer. An ideal plant for the middle to back of a mixed border, given room for its spreading habit.

Height × spread: 1.2 × 2m/4 × 6ft

Soil: Best grown in fertile, moist but well drained soil.

Position: Well suited to a position in full sun. Either grow as a specimen or place within a mixed or shrub border.

Care: As it flowers on the current season's growth, prune hard back to new shoots in spring. Keep well watered until established.

○ ◊ ❄❄❄

95

Photinia × *fraseri* 'Red Robin'

Generally regarded as being frost-hardy in colder areas, this handsome, evergreen shrub is largely grown for its glossy, dark green leaves which, when young, are coloured red or bronze. In mid and late summer small white flowers are produced. An excellent shrub for year-round interest and one which may be relied upon to brighten dull areas.

Height × spread: 5 × 5m/15 × 15ft

Soil: Best grown in fertile, moist but well drained soil.

Position: Well suited to a position in sun or partial shade. Either grow as a specimen or place within a mixed or shrub border.

Care: No regular pruning required. Remove any dead, damaged or unwanted growth over winter. Keep well watered until established, and protect from cold winds.

○ ◑ | ◊ | E | ❄❄

Phygelius aequalis **'Yellow Trumpet'**: Cape figwort

A frost-hardy, semi-evergreen or evergreen shrub which is best treated as an herbaceous perennial in all but the warmest of areas and cut down to ground level each spring. Pale creamy-yellow, trumpet-shaped flowers are produced in hanging heads over light green leaves throughout the summer into autumn. Another form, *P. aequalis* 'Winchester Fanfare', produces attractive, dusky-pink flowers.

Height × spread: 1 × 1m/3 × 3ft

Soil: Best grown in fertile, moist but well drained soil.

Position: Well suited to a position in full sun. Place as required in the herbaceous or mixed border or appropriate garden situation.

Care: In all but the warmest of areas cut back stems to new shoots at ground level in spring. Keep well watered until established.

◑ ◊ E ❋❋

Prunus lusitanica: Portugese laurel

In extremes of cold this most versatile, evergreen shrub or tree may not prove to be totally hardy. However, it is of immense use in the garden for the way in which the shiny leaves of dark green may be clipped into any shape. In early summer racemes of scented white flowers are produced.

Height × spread: 6–10 × 5m/20–33 × 16ft

Soil: Best grown in fertile, moist but well drained soil.

Position: Well suited to a position in sun or partial shade. Either grow as a specimen or place within a mixed or shrub border.

Care: No regular pruning required. Remove any dead, damaged or unwanted growth over winter. Keep well watered until established.

○ ◑ | ◊ | E | ❋❋❋ (borderline)

Prunus 'Taihaku': Great white cherry

Although the flowering period of this hardy, deciduous cherry is, unfortunately, only fleeting, it is certainly worth growing for that brief time spell. In mid-spring a mature tree carries clusters of pure white flowers borne in profusion over newly emerging leaves of bronze. Of spreading habit, the branches develop in outstretched layers.

Height × spread: 7.5 × 10m/25 × 33ft

Soil: Best grown in fertile, moist but well drained soil.

Position: Well suited to a position in full sun. Either grow as a specimen or place within a mixed or shrub border.

Care: No regular pruning is required. Cut out any unwanted branches over winter. Keep well watered until established.

◯ ◊ ✳✳✳

Prunus tenella 'Firehill'

An ideal, hardy deciduous shrub for the smaller garden. This member of the cherry family forms an upright bush which, in mid and late spring, is massed with clusters of very deep pink flowers. Leaves are of a shiny dark green. It is well suited to the mixed border, and even a single planting of this shrub will help it seem furnished in spring.

Height × spread: 1.5 × 1.5m/5 × 5ft

Soil: Best grown in fertile, moist but well drained soil.

Position: Well suited to a position in full sun. Either grow as a specimen or place within a mixed or shrub border.

Care: Resents all forms of pruning. Cut out any dead branches over winter. Keep well watered until established.

◖ ◊ ✳✳✳

This hardy, deciduous shrub is very different from those flowering currants which are most frequently grown. In late winter and early spring the arching stems carry racemes of green-yellow flowers over leathery leaves of deep green. Later these are followed by red fruits which ripen to black. Well worth seeking out.

Height × spread: 1 × 1.5m/3 × 5ft

Soil: Best grown in fertile, moist but well drained soil.

Position: Well suited to a position in partial shade. Either grow as a specimen or place within a mixed or shrub border.

Care: No regular pruning required. Remove any dead, damaged or unwanted growth over winter. Keep well watered until established.

◑ ◇ ✱✱✱

Rosa 'Fritz Nobis': Rose

Enjoy this hardy shrub rose for its very pretty, lightly scented, semi-double flowers of pale pink throughout the summer. The leaves are of a shiny, deep green and the whole shrub carries attractive heps in autumn. Its habit is upright although the growth is branching. All shrub roses associate well with the pastel shades of lavender and catmint and may be used to host late flowering clematis.

Height × spread: 1.5 × 1.2m/5 × 4ft

Soil: Best grown in humus-rich, moist but well drained soil.

Position: Well suited to a position in full sun. Either grow as a specimen or place within a mixed or shrub border.

Care: No regular pruning required. Remove any dead, damaged or unwanted growth over winter. Keep well watered until established.

◐ ◊ ❄❄❄

Beautifully scented, large, thickly double, creamy-lemon flowers tinged with green make this climbing rose a very desirable addition to the garden. It flowers once only in early to midsummer. It is a vigorous grower and the lower stems may become gaunt.

Height × spread: Climbing to 6m/20ft or more.

Soil: For any well drained, previously enriched soil.

Position: Suitable to grow against a wall, to cover a pergola, arch, or trellis or to be trained around an appropriate support.

Care: Remove dead, diseased or weak growth in early spring. Cut hard back sideshoots that have flowered. Tie in strong new shoots as they develop. Lightly fork in a handful of bonemeal or similar on the surface of the soil around the shrub in spring. Apply a mulch of well rotted manure.

The appeal of this slow growing, hardy, deciduous shrub is the way in which bare stems carry fat, silver-grey catkins in spring before the emergence of the leaves of bright green. These stems, most apparent in winter, are of dark brown-black. The shrub is very attractive when grown close to water.

Height × spread: 1.5 × 1.5m/5 × 5ft

Soil: Best grown in fertile, moisture retentive soil which is not allowed to dry out.

Position: Well suited to a position in sun or partial shade. Either grow as a specimen or place within a mixed or shrub border.

Care: No regular pruning required. Remove any dead, damaged or unwanted growth over winter. Keep well watered until established.

◐ ◑ | ◊ | ❊❊❊

Sarcococca hookeriana var. *digyna*: Sweet box

This hardy, evergreen shrub is of suckering habit with attractive, tapering leaves of a deep green. Throughout the winter it carries clusters of highly scented flowers of creamy-white which, in turn, are followed by black fruits. Excellent when placed alongside a much frequented path where the perfume in season may be readily appreciated.

Height × spread: 1.5 × 2m/5 × 6ft

Soil: Best grown in fertile, moist but well drained soil.

Position: Well suited to a position in sun or partial shade. Either grow as a specimen or place within a mixed or shrub border.

Care: No regular pruning required. Remove any dead, damaged or unwanted growth over winter. Keep well watered until established.

○ ◑ △ E ❄❄❄

Skimmia × *confusa* 'Kew Green'

This hardy, evergreen shrub deserves to be more widely grown not least for its free flowering habit. For a prolonged period in late winter and early spring, panicles of creamy flowers are carried over aromatic leaves of mid-green. Because of its compact habit, it is well suited to the smaller garden.

Height × spread: 1.2 × 1.2m/4 × 4ft

Soil: Best grown in fertile, moist but well drained soil.

Position: Well suited to a position in sun or partial shade. Either grow as a specimen or place within a mixed or shrub border.

Care: No regular pruning required. Remove any dead, damaged or unwanted growth over winter. Keep well watered until established.

| ◐ ◑ | ◊ | E | ✳✳✳ |

Syringa × *persica*: Persian lilac

A hardy, deciduous shrub which is well suited to a situation where a larger lilac would be out of place. This compact form carries beautifully scented, lilac-pink flowers in spring and, although not in such profusion, again in late summer and early autumn. A lovely addition to any garden, and particularly valuable in a small one.

Height × spread: 2 × 2m/6 × 6ft

Soil: Best grown in fertile, moist but well drained, neutral to alkaline soil.

Position: Well suited to a position in sun or partial shade. Either grow as a specimen or place within a mixed or shrub border.

Care: No regular pruning required. Lightly prune when the first flowers of spring are spent. Keep well watered until established.

○ ◑ | ◊ | ❋ ❋ ❋

Taxus baccata: Yew

Although it will make a sizeable tree over many years, yew is most often employed in a garden situation as hedging where its satisfying, deep green, evergreen leaves may be clipped annually to form what is, arguably, the finest of all hedges, especially as a background to a border. If required it may be used for topiary, as it is tolerant of extreme clipping.

Height × spread: 10–20 × 7.5–10m/33–70 × 25–33ft as a tree.

Soil: Best grown in fertile, moist but well drained soil.

Position: Well suited to a position in sun or partial shade. Either grow as a specimen tree or plant as a hedge.

Care: No regular pruning required. As a hedge or topiary, clip to shape in late summer. Keep well watered until established.

○ ◑ ◊ E ❄❄❄

Viburnum bodnantense 'Dawn'

Scent from this lovely, hardy, deciduous shrub will fill an enclosed space in winter and early spring when clusters of tubular, rose-pink flowers appear on bare wood to be followed by occasional blue-black or purple fruits. The leaves emerge bronze in spring and mature to deep green. Plant this shrub as a centrepiece of a winter border.

Height × spread: 3 × 2m/10 × 6ft

Soil: Best grown in fertile, moist but well drained soil.

Position: Well suited to a position in sun or partial shade. Either grow as a specimen or place within a mixed or shrub border.

Care: No regular pruning required. Remove any dead, damaged or unwanted growth over winter. Keep well watered until established.

◐ ◑ | ◊ | ❀ ❀ ❀

Viburnum plicatum 'Mariesii'

One of the main attractions of this hardy, deciduous shrub is the way in which the branches are arranged on a mature specimen as a series of tiers. In late spring they carry saucer-shaped, white flowers which combine with handsome leaves of deep green, turning red-purple in autumn. Very occasionally fruits will develop.

Height × spread: 3 × 4m/10 × 13ft

Soil: Best grown in fertile, moist but well drained soil.

Position: Well suited to a position in sun or partial shade. Either grow as a specimen or place within a mixed or shrub border.

Care: No regular pruning required. Remove any dead, damaged or unwanted growth over winter. Keep well watered until established.

Yucca gloriosa: Spanish dagger

Use this frost-hardy shrub to create a focal point in a Mediterranean or gravel garden where it will thrive in the free draining conditions. Evergreen, lance-shaped, fiercely pointed leaves of blue-green, later deep green, are topped by panicles of white, bell-shaped flowers carried on stout stems from late summer to autumn. An exotic addition to the garden.

Height × **spread:** 2 × 2m/6 × 6ft

Soil: Best grown in any thoroughly well drained soil.

Position: Well suited to a position in full sun. Either grow as a specimen or place within a mixed or shrub border.

Care: No regular pruning required. Remove any dead, damaged or unwanted growth over winter. Keep well watered until established.

E ❄❄

2.
PERENNIALS, BULBS and ANNUALS

Acanthus spinosissimus: Bear's breeches

This stately perennial has bold, spiny, heavily-toothed dark green foliage which, in late summer, is topped by large, showy, purple hooded bracts. Excellent as a late season performer. An upright, strong grower which requires no staking, its form making it a good choice for growing simply as an effective foliage plant.

Height × spread: 1.2m x 75cm/4 x 2½ft

Soil: Best grown in fertile, moist but well drained soil.

Position: Well suited to a position in sun or partial shade. Place as required in the herbaceous or mixed border or appropriate garden situation.

Care: Cut down current season's growth completely to ground level after flowering or in the early spring. Keep well watered until established.

◐ ◑ | ◊ | ❄❄❄

Achillea millefolium 'Lilac Beauty': Yarrow

This long flowering herbaceous perennial is a mainstay of the mixed border, flowering from midsummer until autumn. Attractive pale lilac, flat-topped flowerheads are carried above feathery, light green, deeply cut foliage. A lax grower, it is a wonderful filler amongst other, bolder herbaceous plants. Other good cultivars of *A. millefolium* are 'Cerise Queen' and 'Paprika'.

Height × spread: 1m × 60cm/3 × 2ft

Soil: Best grown in fertile, moist but well drained soil.

Position: Well suited to a position in sun or partial shade. Place as required in the herbaceous or mixed border or appropriate garden situation.

Care: Cut down current season's growth completely to ground level after flowering or in the early spring. Keep well watered until established.

◖◗ | ◊ | ❋❋❋

Aconitum carmichaelii 'Barker's Variety': Monkshood

This late flowering herbaceous perennial has dark green, deeply cut foliage and carries large, intense indigo-blue flowers in late summer. A strikingly beautiful plant, it is an outstanding, reliable performer. All parts of the plant are poisonous and this contributes to the slightly sinister appearance of this beguilingly attractive perennial.

Height × spread: 1.5m × 30cm/5 × 1ft

Soil: Best grown in fertile, moist but well drained soil.

Position: Well suited to a position in sun or partial shade. Place as required in the herbaceous or mixed border or appropriate garden situation.

Care: Cut down current season's growth completely to ground level after flowering or in the early spring. Keep well watered until established.

Agapanthus **Headbourne Hybrid**: African lily

A fairly hardy form, this plant remains in most gardens reliably perennial. Stunning, globular heads of huge blue flowers are held stiffly above strap-like, mid-green leaves in midsummer to give a wonderfully tropical atmosphere. Although entirely suitable as border plants, they can be grown very successfully in containers.

Height × spread: 60 x 45cm/2 x 1¹/₂ft

Soil: Best grown in fertile, moist but well drained soil.

Position: Well suited to a position in full sun but tolerant of some shade. Place as required in the herbaceous or mixed border or appropriate garden situation.

Care: Cut down current season's growth completely to ground level after flowering or in the early spring. Keep well watered until established.

◯◑ ◇ ❋❋/❋❋❋

Ajuga reptans 'Catlin's Giant': Bugle

A spring flowering perennial which makes excellent ground cover. Large leaves of metallic purple are topped by enormous dark blue flowerheads over a prolonged period. The shade of this bold, plummy foliage is effective in combination with other perennials, particularly those with grey or silver foliage.

Height × spread: 15 × 60cm/6in × 2ft

Soil: Best grown in fertile, moist but well drained soil.

Position: Well suited to a position in sun or partial shade. Place as required in the herbaceous or mixed border or appropriate garden situation.

Care: Dead head after flowering to encourage new flowers late in the season. No regular pruning is required. Thinning every two to three years encourages healthy growth.

◐● | ◊ | Semi-E | ❋❋❋

Alchemilla mollis: Lady's mantle

A clump forming perennial which produces massed sprays of limy-yellow flowers from early spring to autumn. Without equal for its reliable flowering, attractive grey-green foliage and disease free nature. It combines well with many other herbaceous perennials contributing a full look to the mixed border. Dead-head immediately to prevent enthusiastic self-seeding.

Height × spread: 60 × 60cm/2 × 2ft

Soil: Best grown in fertile, moist but well drained soil. Tolerant of dry conditions.

Position: Well suited to a position in sun or partial shade. Place as required in the herbaceous or mixed border or appropriate garden situation.

Care: Cut down current season's growth completely to ground level after flowering or in the early spring. Keep well watered until established.

◐ ◑ | ◊ | ✳✳✳

Allium aflatunense '**Purple Sensation**': Onion

A splendid bulb-forming perennial flowering in early summer as an ornamental onion. Rich purple, globular heads balance as if by magic on thin green stalks where, placed to soar above other low growing perennials, they appear outstanding. Taking up very little border space, a huge number may be grown together to great effect.

Height × spread: 1.2m × 30cm/4 × 1ft

Soil: Best grown in fertile and well drained soil.

Position: Well suited to a position in sun or partial shade. Place as required in the herbaceous or mixed border or appropriate garden situation.

Care: Plant the bulbs in autumn. Cut down current season's growth completely to ground level after flowering or in the early spring.

◯◑ △ ❉❉❉

Alstroemeria ligtu hybrids

An exotic addition to the 'hot' border, this frost-hardy perennial makes a wonderful show. Clumps of strap-like leaves and striking flowers in a wide range of bright colours, including a white, pink, yellow, purple and red, are produced throughout the summer. Many named forms are now available although generally they are less hardy than the ligtu hybrids.

Height × spread: 60 × 30cm/2 × 1ft

Soil: For fertile, moist but well drained soil. Tolerant of dry conditions.

Position: Well suited to a position in full sun. Place as required in the herbaceous or mixed border or appropriate garden situation.

Care: Cut down current season's growth completely to ground level after flowering or in the early spring. Keep well watered until established. Protect in winter.

Anemone appenina: Windflower

One of the delights of spring. If the rhizomes are left
undisturbed, then this is an easy perennial to establish
and should, in a semi-shaded situation, naturalize. Mainly
blue, but occasionally white, the flowers appear in spring,
the whole plant becoming dormant by summer. Lovely in
a woodland situation or as an underplanting to deciduous
shrubs.

Height × **spread:** 20 × 30cm/8in × 1ft

Soil: Best grown in fertile, moist but well drained soil.

Position: Well suited to a position in partial shade. Place as required
in the herbaceous or mixed border or appropriate garden situation.

Care: Allow foliage and flowers to die down naturally. Apply a top
dressing of garden compost or similar in autumn.

◐ ◊ ✴✴✴

121

Anemone × *hybrida* 'Honorine Jobert': Japanese anemone

A perennial form of Japanese anemone which has large white single flowers with prominent yellow stamens in late summer and autumn. It is valuable for its long season in bloom and for the colour which it can provide at a time which might otherwise be considered dull. Continuous dead heading will produce a steady supply of new, fresh flowerheads over the dark green lobed foliage.

Height × spread: 1.5m/5ft × indefinite spread

Soil: Best grown in fertile, moist but well drained soil.

Position: Well suited to a position in sun or partial shade. Place as required in the herbaceous or mixed border or appropriate garden situation.

Care: Cut down current season's growth completely to ground level after flowering or in the early spring. Keep well watered until established.

Anemone × *hybrida* **'Pamina'**: Japanese anemone

Double magenta-pink flowers formed from late summer to autumn make this perennial a stylish choice for the late season herbaceous border. An attractive, easy natured plant which prolongs the flowering interest of the garden well into autumn. It combines well with a wide range of other late perennials and looks especially good when placed among repeat flowering roses.

Height × spread: 1.5m/5ft × indefinite spread

Soil: Best grown in fertile, moist but well drained soil.

Position: Well suited to a position in sun or partial shade. Place as required in the herbaceous or mixed border or appropriate garden situation.

Care: Cut down current season's growth completely to ground level after flowering or in the early spring. Keep well watered until established.

◐ ◑ | ◊ | ❋❋❋

Aquilegia 'Magpie': Columbine

An unusual form of this easy, well-loved perennial which has near black and white flowers carried in abundance above purple-tinged foliage of mid-green. An excellent plant for creating a sombre atmosphere in the border and looks well in combination with other deep purple plants such as *Anthriscus sylvestris* 'Ravenswing' or plum flowered hellebores. A prolific self-seeder, it will cross with other aquilegias if they are planted in close proximity.

Height × spread: 60 × 45cm/2 × 1¹/₂ft

Soil: Best grown in fertile, moist but well drained soil.

Position: Suitable for sun or partial shade. Tolerant of deeper shade where soil remains moist.

Care: Cut down the current season's growth to ground level immediately after flowering; new foliage will remain looking good over winter.

○ ◐ | ◇ | ❄❄❄

Arctotis × *hybrida* 'Apricot': African daisy

A frost-tender perennial to give a splash of colour to summer borders. Available in shades of red, white, yellow, or apricot as here, the African daisies flower from early summer to the first frosts. Regular deadheading encourages new flowers to be produced, prolonging the display. The leaves are a silvery-green.

Height × **spread:** 45 × 30cm/1¹/₂ × 1ft

Soil: Best grown in fertile, moist but well drained soil.

Position: Well suited to a position in full sun. Place as required in the herbaceous or mixed border or appropriate garden situation.

Care: Not winter hardy. In cold areas propagate from cuttings in late summer and overwinter in a frost free glasshouse. Alternatively, dig up, pot and protect from frost.

An outstanding perennial which is deservedly popular for its long flowering period and mildew resistance. An abundance of single, lilac flowers are produced above the dark green leaves from midsummer through until autumn. This plant associates well with a huge range of perennials, including agastaches and phloxes, and adds considerably to the late season border.

Height × spread: 75 × 45cm/2¹/₂ × 1¹/₂ft

Soil: Best grown in fertile, moist but well drained soil.

Position: Well suited to a position in sun or partial shade. Place as required in the herbaceous or mixed border or appropriate garden situation.

Care: Cut down current season's growth completely to ground level after flowering or in the early spring. Keep well watered until established.

◯ ◑ | ◊ | ✳✳✳

Baptisia australis: False indigo

Dark indigo, pea-like flowers produced from spring to early summer make this perennial a charming and unusual addition to the herbaceous border. Excellent in combination with the lemon-yellow flowers of other perennials, it is well worth obtaining. Slow to develop, *B. australis* is a good choice for a small garden.

Height × spread: 75 × 60cm/2¹/₂ × 2ft

Soil: Best grown in fertile, moist but well drained soil.

Position: Well suited to a position in sun or partial shade. Place as required in the herbaceous or mixed border or appropriate garden situation. .

Care: Cut down current season's growth completely to ground level after flowering or in the early spring. Keep well watered until established.

○ ◑ | ◊ | ❄❄❄

Bergenia purpurascens: Elephant's ears

In winter the leaves of this handsome, evergreen perennial are a glowing papal purple. As the days warm, they will revert to green and produce richly coloured flowers in spring of a deep pink. Other varieties are available which produce white or paler pink flowers and a range of leaf shapes and forms. *B. cordifolia* 'Purpurea' also has purple leaves in winter.

Height × spread: 30 × 45cm/1 × 1½ft

Soil: Best grown in fertile, moist but well drained soil.

Position: Well suited to a position in sun or partial shade. Place as required in the herbaceous or mixed border or appropriate garden situation.

Care: Remove spent flowerheads and dead leaves to keep the plant looking good all year round.

○ ◑ | ◊ | E | ❋❋❋

Brunnera macrophylla 'Dawson's White': Siberian bugloss

A reliable perennial for the spring border, this is a good form which has, unusually, thick creamy-white margins to the broad, mid-green leaves and occasionally leaves are entirely cream. Forget-me-not blue flowers are produced in abundant sprays from early spring to summer, the foliage remaining attractive for even longer.

Height × spread: 45 × 45cm/1¹/₂ × 1¹/₂ft

Soil: Best grown in fertile, moist but well drained soil.

Position: Well suited to a position in partial or full shade. Place as required in the herbaceous or mixed border or appropriate garden situation.

Care: Remove spent flowers and any dead leaves to keep the plant looking good. Cut down current season's growth completely to ground level in autumn.

◐ ● | ◊ | ✳✳✳

Bupleurum angulosum

Rarely seen and, sadly, difficult to obtain, this all green perennial has intriguing astrantia-like flowerheads formed on thin, wiry stems. Flowering in midsummer, the aquamarine, strap-like leaves, topped by pale green, pincushion flowers, make an attractive and unusual sight. As the flowerheads mature, so prominent shiny black seeds are formed.

Height × spread: 60 × 30cm/2 × 1ft

Soil: Best grown in fertile, moist but well drained soil.

Position: Well suited to a position in full sun. Place as required in the herbaceous or mixed border or appropriate garden situation.

Care: Cut down current season's growth completely to ground level after flowering or in the early spring. Keep well watered until established.

◯ | ◊ | ❄❄❄

Caltha palustris: Marsh marigold

This moisture-loving perennial carries waxy flowers of deep butter-yellow in spring over dark green, kidney-shaped leaves. It is an attractive plant which, on account of the vibrancy of its flowers, brings cheer to the garden after the long, often drear days of winter. Looks well in association with water. There is also a double-flowered form in cultivation.

Height × spread: 45 × 45cm/1½ × 1½ft

Soil: Best grown in fertile, moisture retentive soil which is not allowed to dry out.

Position: Well suited to a position in sun or partial shade. Place as required in the bog garden, at the pond or streamside or in an appropriate garden situation.

Care: Cut down current season's growth completely to ground level after flowering or in the early spring before flowers and leaves emerge.

◐◑ ◊ ❋❋❋

Camassia leichtlinii subsp. *suksdorfii*: Quamash

A frost-hardy, moisture-loving bulbous perennial flowering in spring when slender stalks of pale green soar above rush-like foliage carrying a mass of deep blue flowers. It is highly effective when grown near water or when allowed to naturalize in grass. *C. leichtlinii* itself has creamy-white flowers. The leaves of these plants die down after flowering.

Height × spread: 75 × 30cm/2½ × 1ft

Soil: Best grown in fertile, moisture retentive soil which is not allowed to dry out.

Position: Well suited to a position in sun or partial shade. Place as required in the herbaceous or mixed border or appropriate garden situation.

Care: Cut down the spent growth completely to ground level after flowering. Keep well watered until established.

◯◑◐ ◊ ❋❋

Campanula lactiflora: Milky bellflower

A tall perennial producing bell-shaped flowers of white or lavender-blue, or soft pink in the form 'Loddon Anna', through summer into autumn. An easy but impressive plant which adds height to the herbaceous border, generally without the need for staking. Allowed to set seed it will gently seed around to produce extra plants for the new season.

Height × spread: 1.2m × 60cm/4 × 2ft

Soil: Best grown in fertile, moist but well drained soil.

Position: Well suited to a position in sun or partial shade. Place as required in the herbaceous or mixed border or apporpriate garden situation.

Care: Cut down current season's growth completely to ground level after flowering or in the early spring. Keep well watered until established.

Campanula latiloba alba: Bellflower

A strong growing, clump forming perennial whose basal rosettes of mid-green leaves produce tall stems of cup-shaped, pure white flowers in mid and late summer. Without equal as an easy, disease-free plant which is reliably free flowering whatever the season's conditions. The type plant has violet-blue flowers. 'Hidcote Amethyst' is a soft lilac.

Height × spread: 1m × 45cm/3 × 1 1/2ft

Soil: Best grown in fertile, moist but well drained soil.

Position: Well suited to a position in sun or partial shade. Place as required in the herbaceous or mixed border or appropriate garden situation.

Care: Cut down current season's growth completely to ground level after flowering or in the early spring. Keep well watered until established.

Campanula punctata 'Rubriflora': Bellflower

An unusual form of bellflower which forms a vigorous, creeping perennial flowering in early summer. The large, hanging bells of dusky pink flowers, crimson spotted within each bloom, add a dramatic touch to the herbaceous border and make an excellent contrast to other low growing border plants. It forms rosettes of dark green leaves.

Height × spread: 30 × 45cm/1 × 1¹/₂ft

Soil: Best grown in fertile, moist but well drained soil.

Position: Well suited to a position in sun or partial shade. Place as required in the herbaceous or mixed border or appropriate garden situation.

Care: Cut down current season's growth completely to ground level after flowering or in the early spring. Keep well watered until established.

◐ ◑ │ ◊ │ ✳ ✳ ✳

Cardamine pratensis 'Flore Pleno': Lady's smock

This exceedingly charming double flowering form of the perennial lady's smock has been in cultivation for many centuries. An understated perennial with double flowers of pale lilac-pink emerging from a clump of pale green, ferny foliage in spring. Unlike the single-flowered form, this cultivar is neat and not invasive in any garden position.

Height × spread: 20 × 30cm/8in × 1ft

Soil: Best grown in fertile, moisture retentive soil which is not allowed to dry out.

Position: Well suited to a position in sun or partial shade. Place as required in the herbaceous or mixed border or appropriate garden situation.

Care: Cut down current season's growth completely to ground level after flowering or in the early spring. Keep well watered until established.

○ ◑ ◐ | ❋❋❋

136

Centaurea macrocephala: Knapweed

Notwithstanding somewhat coarse leaves, this tall border perennial is an excellent addition to any scheme calling for a bold treatment. Rich butter-yellow flowers open from brown papery bracts in early summer to remain constant for several weeks. Later the flowerheads may be dried and arranged indoors. It is especially effective when grown with the rose, *Rosa* 'Graham Thomas', with golden double flowers.

Height × spread: 1m × 60cm/3 × 2ft

Soil: Best grown in fertile, moist but well drained soil.

Position: Well suited to a position in sun or partial shade. Place as required in the herbaceous or mixed border or appropriate garden situation.

Care: Cut down current season's growth completely to ground level after flowering or in the early spring. Keep well watered until established.

◐◑ ◊ ❄❄❄

Centaurea montana alba: Knapweed

A superior form, this perennial has the most wonderful decoratively presented foliage topped by elegant flowerheads of the purest white produced from late spring to midsummer, held on woolly stems. The pale mid-green leaves are felted white and positively glisten on sunny days. Regular dead heading will prolong flowering for months.

Height × spread: 45 × 60cm/1¹/₂ × 2ft

Soil: Best grown in fertile, moist but well drained soil.

Position: Well suited to a position in sun or partial shade. Place as required in the herbaceous or mixed border or appropriate garden situation.

Care: Cut down current season's growth completely to ground level after flowering or in the early spring. Keep well watered until established.

◐ ◑ | ⬦ | ❋❋❋

Cephalaria gigantea: Giant scabious

A splendid, tall growing border perennial which always attracts attention. Soft primrose-yellow, scabious-type flowers are held high on statuesque stems above mid-green, cut-leafed foliage in midsummer to give a dramatic and stately effect. Allow to seed around gently to produce additional plants for the coming year. It is vigorous and will form a large clump.

Height × spread: 2 × 1.2m/6 × 4ft

Soil: For fertile, moist but well drained soil. Tolerant of dry conditions.

Position: Well suited to a position in sun or partial shade. Place as required in the herbaceous or mixed border or appropriate garden situation.

Care: Cut down current season's growth completely to ground level after flowering or in the early spring. Keep well watered until established.

In early spring the starry blue flowers of this bulbous perennial are a magical sight among the small strap-like leaves. The white centres of the flowers positively glow and lift the spirits even on the dullest of days. Mixing well amongst early spring bulbs, this plant is well suited to the front of border or rock garden. A white form called *C. l.* 'Alba' is available but in limited supply.

Height: 10cm/4in

Soil: Best grown in fertile, moist but well drained soil.

Position: Well suited to a position in sun or partial shade. Place as required in the herbaceous or mixed border or appropriate garden situation.

Care: Allow foliage and flowers to die down naturally. Apply a top dressing of garden compost or similar in autumn.

◐ ◑ | ◊ | ✳✳✳

Cirsium rivulare 'Atropurpureum'

A strikingly different perennial with dark green, thistle-like leaves and pincushion flowerheads of the deepest crimson produced in summer. Grown to best effect amongst silver or plummy coloured foliage, this plant is bound to attract attention. Rather than sowing seed, increase by division, if you want to keep this excellent form of cirsium true to colour.

Height × spread: 1.2m × 60cm/4 × 2ft

Soil: Best grown in fertile, moisture retentive soil which is not allowed to dry out.

Position: Well suited to a position in full sun. Place as required in the herbaceous or mixed border or appropriate garden situation.

Care: Cut down current season's growth completely to ground level after flowering or in the early spring. Keep well watered until established.

○ ◐ | ❋❋❋

Convallaria majalis: Lily-of-the-valley

A rhizomatous perennial which spreads steadily and is excellent as ground cover, particularly in shade. Sweetly scented, white bell-shaped flowers are produced in late spring on leafless stems. No garden should be without this understated yet traditional harbinger of spring. There are other forms, including a pink-flowered, or a double-flowered cultivar, and one with striped leaves.

Height × spread: 25 × 30cm/10in × 1ft

Soil: Best grown in fertile, moist but well drained soil.

Position: Well suited to a position in partial or full shade. Place as required in the herbaceous or mixed border or appropriate garden situation.

Care: Cut down current season's growth completely to ground level in autumn. Keep young plants well watered until established.

◐ ● | ◊ | ❋❋❋

Cosmos atrosanguineus: Chocolate flower

Although frost hardy, this perennial is well worth cultivating for its amazing rich ruby flowers strongly smelling of hot chocolate. The open cup-shaped flowers with dark brown central discs are produced in profusion from midsummer to autumn and are held on wiry dark stems above dark green foliage. It is sometimes grown as a container plant, dramatic amongst silver foliage.

Height × spread: 75 × 45cm/2½ × 1½ft

Soil: Best grown in fertile, moist but well drained soil.

Position: Well suited to a position in full sun. Place as required in the herbaceous or mixed border or appropriate garden situation.

Care: Not totally winter hardy. In cold areas propagate from cuttings in late summer and overwinter in a frost free glasshouse. Otherwise lift, pot and protect from frost.

143

Crambe cordifolia

An impressive perennial with large, dark green leaves from which erupts a cloud of many-branched panicles of dainty white scented flowers from late spring to midsummer. A wonderful sight in the herbaceous border and a useful plant with which to disguise the dying foliage and flowers of earlier flowering perennials.

Height × spread: 2.4 × 1.5m/8 × 5ft

Soil: Best grown in fertile, moist but well drained soil.

Position: Well suited to a position in full sun. Place as required in the herbaceous or mixed border or appropriate garden situation.

Care: Cut down current season's growth completely to ground level after flowering or in the early spring. Keep well watered until established.

◯ ◊ ✲✲✲

Crinum × *powellii*

A deciduous, bulbous perennial with long, strap-like leaves of pale green and huge heads of mid-pink, trumpet-shaped flowers. Flowering from late summer into autumn, the scent produced can be overwhelming. A beautiful and graceful addition to any herbaceous or mixed border. There is also a white form called *C.* × *powellii* 'Album'.

Height × spread: 1.5m × 30cm/5 × 1ft

Soil: Best grown in fertile, humus-rich, moist but well drained soil.

Position: Well suited to a position in full sun. Place as required in the herbaceous or mixed border or appropriate garden situation.

Care: Allow foliage and flowers to die down naturally. Apply a top dresing of garden compost or similar at a time when bulbs are dormant.

145

Crocosmia 'Severn Sunrise': Montbretia

An outstanding form of this frost-hardy perennial with glowing salmon-orange flowerheads produced in profusion from late summer to autumn. The fresh green, sword-like leaves give a pleasing contrast to the sprays of flowerheads, the whole plant making a bold statement and a tremendous splash of colour in the herbaceous border.

Height × spread: 1m × 8cm/3ft × 3in

Soil: Best grown in fertile, moist but well drained soil.

Position: Well suited to a position in sun or partial shade. Place as required in the herbaceous or mixed border or appropriate garden situation.

Care: Cut down current season's growth completely to ground level after flowering or in the early spring. Keep well watered until established.

◐◑ ◊ ❅❅

Crocosmia 'Vulcan': Montbretia

A frost hardy, cormous perennial which is very valuable for its end of season display of crimson-red flowers. The bright green, lance-shaped leaves are topped by arching stems of tubular flowers produced in late summer. Heavy mulching in winter is necessary to protect the corms.

Height × spread: 1m × 8cm/3ft × 3in

Soil: Best grown in fertile, moist but well drained soil.

Position: Well suited to a position in sun or partial shade. Place as required in the herbaceous or mixed border or appropriate garden situation.

Care: Cut down current season's growth completely to ground level after flowering or in the early spring. Keep well watered until established.

Crocus tommasinianus

A cormous perennial with goblet-shaped flowers of pale
lilac produced from late winter to spring. Drifts naturalized
in short grass make a truly amazing sight that is, sadly, all
too brief. No garden should be without this crocus to herald
the start of the gardening year, but if introduced into a
herbaceous border they may become invasive.

Height × spread: 10 × 5cm/4 × 2in

Soil: Best grown in fertile, moist but well drained soil.

Position: Well suited to a position in sun or partial shade. Place as
required in the herbaceous or mixed border or appropriate garden
situation.

Care: Allow foliage and flowers to die down naturally. Apply a top
dressing of garden compost or similar in autumn.

○ ◑ | ◊ | ✳✳✳

This tuberous perennial is a real treasure of autumn.
Valuable for its distinctive, triangular-shaped leaves,
tinged purple, produced after its display of delicate
flowers in all shades of pink (or white in the form of *C.h.*
f. *album*) which emerge from late summer into autumn.
Other forms of cyclamen can be grown to flower all
through the year.

Height × spread: 10 × 15cm/4 × 6in

Soil: Best grown in fertile, moist but well drained soil.

Position: Well suited to a position in sun or partial shade. Place as
required in the herbaceous or mixed border or appropriate garden
situation.

Care: Allow foliage and flowers to die down naturally. Apply a top
dressing of garden compost or similar as the leaves die.

◐◑ | ◊ | ❈❈❈

Dahlia 'Bishop of Llandaff'

A tuberous, frost hardy perennial with dark, near black foliage and flowerheads of brilliant crimson with bright yellow centres. A show stopper in the herbaceous border flowering from late summer to the frosts, this plant is guaranteed to attract comment. It is excellent as a component in a hot colour scheme.

Height × spread: 60 × 60cm/2 × 2ft

Soil: Best grown in fertile, humus-rich, moist but well drained soil.

Position: Well suited to a position in full sun. Place as required in the herbaceous or mixed border or appropriate garden situation.

Care: Overwinter tubers, after the first frosts, by lifting, drying off and storing in dry peat or sand in a frost-free place.

◐ ◊ ❄❄

Dahlia 'Moonfire'

A tuberous frost-hardy perennial with deeply coloured foliage above which are carried single flowers of soft apricot and vermilion from late summer until the first frosts of winter. One of numerous cultivars, the popularity of which is currently on the increase because of their long-flowering period in the second half of the year.

Height × **spread:** 60 × 60cm/2 × 2ft

Soil: Best grown in fertile, humus-rich, moist but well drained soil.

Position: Well suited to a position in full sun. Place as required in the herbaceous or mixed border or appropriate garden situation.

Care: Overwinter tubers, after the first frosts, by lifting, drying off and storing in dry peat or sand in a frost-free place.

◖ ◊ ❄❄

Delphinium 'Alice Artindale'

All delphiniums make good border plants but this is a highly desirable double form with flowers of an unusual violet-blue. Slow to establish, it is well worth the wait to see the impressive flower spikes borne in early to midsummer complemented by the slatey blue-green leaves. Thoroughly excellent, but as with all tall delphiniums, it is necessary to give some support.

Height × spread: 1.5m × 60cm/5 × 2ft

Soil: Best grown in fertile, moist but well drained soil.

Position: Well suited to a position in full sun. Place as required in the herbaceous or mixed border or appropriate garden situation.

Care: Cut down current season's growth completely to ground level after flowering or in the early spring. Keep well watered until established.

Dianthus 'Pike's Pink': Pink

Border pinks begin their long flowering period in early summer. This charming variety is one of the many suitable for the rock garden or as an edging at the front of a border. Dainty double flowers of shell-pink are produced in profusion from early to midsummer above grey-green, mat-like evergreen foliage. Good drainage and full sun are essential.

Height × spread: 15 × 15cm/6 × 6in

Soil: Best grown in fertile, moist but well drained soil.

Position: Well suited to a position in full sun. Place as required in the herbaceous or mixed border or appropriate garden situation.

Care: Cut down current season's growth completely to ground level after flowering or in the early spring. Keep well watered until established.

◖ ◊ E ❄❄❄

Dicentra 'Bacchanal': Bleeding heart

A spring flowering perennial with finely cut, fern-like, grey-green leaves and hanging heads of deep blood-red flowers. Suitable for the border or rock garden, this easy plant is an absolute joy and is most striking when placed to surround the plum-coloured foliage of *Cotinus* 'Grace'. Spreading by rhizomes, it will form a clump.

Height × spread: 45 × 30cm/1 1/2 × 1ft

Soil: Best grown in humus-rich, moist but well drained alkaline or neutral soil.

Position: Well suited to a position in sun or partial shade. Place as required in the herbaceous or mixed border or appropriate garden situation.

Care: Cut down current season's growth completely to ground level after flowering or in the early spring. Keep well watered until established.

154

Dictamnus albus var. *purpureus*: Burning bush

A woody perennial with lemon-scented leaves and pinky-mauve flowers with darker veining formed in early summer. The common name for this plant comes from its ability to be set alight in hot weather on account of the volatile, aromatic oil contained in the flower stamens and unripened seeds.

Height × spread: 60 × 60cm/2 × 2ft

Soil: Best grown in fertile, moist but well drained soil.

Position: Well suited to a position in sun or partial shade. Place as required in the herbaceous or mixed border or appropriate garden situation.

Care: Cut down current season's growth completely to ground level after flowering or in the early spring. Keep well watered until established.

◐ ◑ | ◌ | ✻✻✻

Digitalis ferruginea: Rusty foxglove

This tall growing biennial or short lived perennial is one of the aristocrats of the foxglove family. Apricot flowers, veined brown-red on the inside, are produced in midsummer in great profusion along the flower stem. The plant which has dark green, lance-like leaves will gently seed around given the right conditions and is tolerant of a varied range of situations.

Height × spread: 1.2m × 45cm/4 × 1¹/₂ft

Soil: Best grown in fertile, moist but well drained soil.

Position: Well suited to a position in partial shade. Place as required in the herbaceous or mixed border or appropriate garden situation.

Care: Cut down current season's growth completely to ground level after flowering or in the early spring. Keep well watered until established.

◑ ◊ ❊❊❊

Flowers of crushed strawberry-pink in late spring and
early summer set this tall-growing perennial apart. The
lance-shaped leaves are of a shiny dark green and are
noticeably, and attractively, veined. It thrives best when
divisions are made every two to three years. An excellent
border plant which deserves to be widely grown.

Height × spread: 1m × 30cm/3 × 1ft

Soil: Best grown in fertile, moist but well drained soil.

Position: Well suited to a position in partial shade. Place as required
in the herbaceous or mixed border or appropriate garden situation.

Care: Cut down current season's growth completely to ground level
after flowering or in the early spring. Keep well watered until
established.

◗ ◊ ❄❄❄

Echinacea purpurea: Cone flower

A tall, upright perennial with large, showy flowerheads of purple-red with a central cone-shaped disc of golden-brown produced from midsummer to early autumn. An excellent plant to combine with other late season performers such as *Verbena bonariensis* and *Eryngium bourgatii*. There is also a beautiful white form that is called 'White Swan', see opposite.

Height × spread: 1.2m × 45cm/4 × 1½ft

Soil: Best grown in fertile, moist but well drained soil.

Position: Well suited to a position in sun but tolerant of partial shade. Place as required in the herbaceous or mixed border or appropriate garden situation.

Care: Cut down current season's growth completely to ground level after flowering or in the early spring. Keep well watered until established.

◐◑ | ◊ | ❋❋❋

Echinacea purpurea 'White Swan': Cone flower

Valuable for its late and extended flowering season from midsummer to early autumn, this perennial carries single daisy-type flowers on stiff stems. The green-white flowerheads with orange-brown central discs create a worthwhile and interesting display in the late season border.

Height × spread: 60 × 45cm/2 × 1¹/₂ft

Soil: Best grown in fertile, moist but well drained soil.

Position: Well suited to a position in sun but tolerant of partial shade. Place as required in the herbaceous or mixed border or appropriate garden situation.

Care: Cut down current season's growth completely to ground level after flowering or in the early spring. Keep well watered until established.

◐◑ ◊ ❋❋❋

A choice, clump forming perennial with pure white flowers in spring. The bronze-coloured young leaves provide an exciting contrast with the flowers to make this a star performer in the early part of the gardening year. It is very suitable because of its compact size for the rock garden.

Height × spread: 25 × 30cm/10in × 1ft

Soil: Best grown in fertile, moist but well drained soil.

Position: Well suited to a position in partial shade. Place as required in the herbaceous or mixed border or appropriate garden situation.

Care: Cut down current season's growth completely to ground level in the early spring before the emergence of flowers. Keep well watered until established.

◐ ◇ ❋❋❋

Eremurus bungei: Foxtail lily

Soaring flower spikes of orange-yellow in early and midsummer create a dramatic display in the herbaceous border. No other plant is capable of such drama at this time of year, particularly when placed against dark green foliage. Guaranteed to create an interesting, rather tropical look to the border. Mulch the young shoots to protect them.

Height × spread: 1.5m × 60cm/5 × 2ft

Soil: Best grown in fertile, free draining, sandy soil.

Position: Well suited to a position in full sun. Place as required in the herbaceous or mixed border or appropriate garden situation.

Care: Cut down current season's growth completely to ground level after flowering or in the early spring. Keep well watered until established.

Erigeron karvinskianus: Fleabane

This short-lived perennial is a low growing, spreading plant which produces tiny buttons of daisy flowers in summer which open white and then fade to pink and purple. Freely self-seeding, once acquired it will continue to appear, often in the most unexpected of places, colonizing rock walls for example or, sometimes, flights of steps or paving cracks.

Height × spread: 15cm × 1m/6in × 3ft

Soil: Best grown in fertile, moist but well drained soil.

Position: Well suited to a position in full sun with some shade during the hottest part of the day. Allow to seed into cracks and crevices.

Care: Cut down current season's growth completely to ground level after flowering once seeding has taken place. Keep well watered until established.

○ ◊ ❊❊❊

From a basal clump of silver-veined, dark green spiny leaves erupt clouds of grey-green flowers on bluish stems in summer. The lustrous, thistle-like flowers of this appealing perennial have an ethereal quality when set among other plants in the herbaceous border. The form *E.b.* 'Oxford Blue' has flower heads of a darker, more pronounced blue.

Height × spread: 60 × 30cm/2 × 1ft

Soil: Best grown in fertile, moist but well drained soil.

Position: Well suited to a position in sun or partial shade. Place as required in the herbaceous or mixed border or appropriate garden situation.

Care: Cut down current season's growth completely to ground level after flowering or in the early spring. Keep well watered until established.

◐ ◑ | ◊ | ❋❋❋

A compact perennial with very appealing, variegated, spiky foliage topped by rounded, thistle-like, pale lilac-blue flowerheads in late summer. A charmingly ethereal and distinctive plant, it is useful for adding texture and form to the herbaceous border, complementing well a wide range of other late-flowering perennials, especially *Echinacea purpurea*.

Height × spread: 45 × 25cm/1¹/₂ft × 10in

Soil: Best grown in fertile, moist but well drained soil.

Position: Well suited to a position in full sun. Place as required in the herbaceous or mixed border or appropriate garden situation.

Care: Cut down current season's growth completely to ground level after flowering or in the early spring. Keep well watered until established.

○ ◊ ❋❋❋

Erythronium 'Pagoda': Dog's tooth violet

An elegant and beautiful bulbous perennial carrying
nodding heads of deep yellow flowers in profusion in
spring. The basal leaves are clump forming and prettily
marbled with white veining. Suitable for the border, rock
garden or alpine house, it increases only slowly. Other
named forms are available with white, lilac or pink
flowers.

Height × spread: 25 × 10cm/10 × 4in

Soil: Best grown in humus-rich, moist but well drained soil.

Position: Well suited to a position in partial shade. Place as required
in the herbaceous or mixed border or appropriate garden situation.

Care: Allow foliage and flowers to die down naturally. Apply a top
dressing of garden compost or similar in autumn.

◑ ◊ ❀❀❀

This bulbous perennial is on the borderline of hardiness but is well worth the extra care needed to grow it well. Striking racemes of starry green-white flowers, spotted purple, are produced in late summer, each topped with a tuft of foliage. A superb specimen plant for a container, but when the flowers first open they have an off-putting smell which is pronounced in a confined area.

Height × spread: 30–60 × 20cm/1–2ft × 8in

Soil: Best grown in fertile, moist but well drained soil.

Position: Well suited to a position in full sun. In cold areas grow in a container and overwinter in a frost free glasshouse.

Care: Allow foliage and flowers to die down naturally. Apply a top dressing of garden compost or similar in autumn.

◯ ◊ ✳✳✳ (borderline)

Euphorbia dulcis 'Chameleon': Spurge

Few plants contribute as much to the herbaceous border as this unassuming form of spurge. The young foliage of this rhizomatous perennial is a wonderful plum-purple and contrasts well with the yellow-green flowerheads produced in early summer. Hard pruning after flowering encourages the continuous production of new leaves.

Height × **spread:** 30 × 30cm/1 × 1ft

Soil: Best grown in fertile, moist but well drained soil.

Position: Well suited to a position in partial shade. Place as required in the herbaceous or mixed border or appropriate garden situation.

Care: Cut down current season's growth completely to ground level in autumn. Keep young plants well watered until established.

◐ ⬡ ✳✳✳

Euphorbia griffithii 'Fireglow': Spurge

Given time, this striking perennial will spread to cover a wide area. In early summer tall stems of orange-red bracts are carried over tapering leaves of reddish-green. Later, at the approach of autumn, foliage colours well. As with all euphorbias, the stems contain a milky sap which may cause irritation to the skin.

Height × spread: 1 × 1m/3 × 3ft

Soil: Best grown in fertile, moist but well drained soil.

Position: Well suited to a position in partial shade. Place as required in the herbaceous or mixed border or appropriate garden situation.

Care: Cut down current season's growth completely to ground level in autumn. Keep young plants well watered until established.

◑ ◊ ❄❄❄

Fritillaria persica: Fritillary

This stately form of fritillary is a tall growing, bulbous perennial. The bell-shaped, dusty purple flowers produced in spring contrast beautifully with the lance-shaped, grey-green leaves. Plant deeply and ensure good drainage. All forms of fritillaria are valuable garden plants and are very varied in shape, size and flower colour.

Height × spread: 1m × 10cm/3ft × 4in

Soil: Best grown in fertile, moist but well drained soil.

Position: Well suited to a position in full sun. Place as required in the herbaceous or mixed border or appropriate garden situation.

Care: Allow foliage and flowers to die down naturally. Apply a top dressing of garden compost or similar in autumn.

| ◯ | ◌ | ❋❋❋ |

169

Galanthus 'Magnet': Snowdrop

No garden can be without snowdrops to lift the curtain on the gardening year. This particularly robust form of bulbous perennial is distinctively marked with a green V on the inner petals of the large white flowers produced in late winter and early spring. The narrow grey-green strap-like leaves should be allowed to die down naturally.

Height × spread: 20 × 8cm/8 × 3in

Soil: Best grown in fertile, moisture retentive soil which is not allowed to dry out.

Position: Well suited to a position in partial shade. Place as required in the herbaceous or mixed border or appropriate garden situation.

Care: Allow foliage and flowers to die down naturally. Apply a top dressing of garden compost or similar in autumn.

◑ ◊ ❄❄❄

Galium odoratum: Sweet woodruff

A spreading perennial which makes excellent ground cover. Bright green leaves are topped by clusters of tiny, starry white flowers on thin stems from late spring to midsummer. A charming, attractive and reliably free flowering plant suitable for growing in a wide range of conditions. Its common English name is a reference to the sweetness of its scent, reminiscent of dried hay.

Height × spread: 30cm/1ft × indefinite spread

Soil: Best grown in fertile, moist but well drained soil.

Position: Well suited to a position in sun or partial shade. Place as required in the herbaceous or mixed border or appropriate garden situation.

Care: Cut down current season's growth completely to ground level after flowering or in the early spring. Keep well watered until established.

◐ ◑ | ◊ | ❄❄❄

Gaura lindheimeri

A clump-forming perennial of elegant habit carrying wands of star-shaped white flowers on slender stems from early summer to early autumn. Contributing a light and airy look to the herbaceous border this plant, which is of American origin, combines readily with a wide range of other perennials and shrubs, and is especially valuable for its extended flowering period.

Height × spread: 1m × 60cm/3 × 2ft

Soil: Best grown in fertile, moist but well drained soil.

Position: Well suited to a position in sun or partial shade. Place as required in the herbaceous or mixed border or appropriate garden situation.

Care: Cut down current season's growth completely to ground level after flowering or in the early spring. Keep well watered until established.

○ ◑ | ◊ | ✱✱✱

Geranium renardii: Cranesbill

An unusual form of cranesbill, this perennial has scalloped, felted leaves of soft grey-green and carries near white flowers, veined with violet, in summer. Cutting back hard after flowering retains the neat, clump-forming shape and encourages new foliage which remains throughout the winter.

Height × spread: 30 × 30cm/1 × 1ft

Soil: Best grown in fertile, moist but well drained soil.

Position: Well suited to a position in full sun. Place as required in the herbaceous or mixed border or appropriate garden situation.

Care: Cut down current season's growth completely to ground level after flowering or in the early spring. Keep well watered until established.

Geranium × riversleaianum 'Mavis Simpson': Cranesbill

A summer-flowering perennial of trailing habit which forms excellent ground cover amongst other herbaceous plants. Pretty, pale pink flowers with paler centres are produced in profusion over grey-green leaves. So many varieties of cranesbill are available that one can be found to suit every situation.

Height × spread: 30cm × 1m/1 × 3ft

Soil: Best grown in fertile, moist but well drained soil.

Position: Well suited to a position in sun or partial shade. Place as required in the herbaceous or mixed border or appropriate garden situation.

Care: Cut down current season's growth completely to ground level after flowering or in the early spring. Keep well watered until established.

Geum rivale 'Album': Avens

A deservedly popular perennial flowering over an
extended period in late spring and summer. The plant has
attractive heads of creamy-white flowers which are
produced prolifically above mid-green leaves. Other forms
of geum include *G.* 'Borisii' with orange-red flowers and
G. 'Red Wings' with semi-double flowers of scarlet, which
bloom in early to midsummer.

Height × spread: 30 × 30cm/1 × 1ft

Soil: For fertile, moisture retentive soil which is not allowed to dry out.

Position: Well suited to a position in sun or partial shade. Place in
the herbaceous or mixed border or appropriate garden situation.

Care: Cut down current season's growth completely to ground level after
flowering or in the early spring. Keep well watered until established.

◐◑ | ◊ | ❋❋❋

Gillenia trifoliata: Indian physic

An upright perennial carrying starry flowers on dark, wiry
stems from late spring to late summer. This is a plant of
delicate appearance which gives the impression of white
moths fluttering, particularly when caught in a light
breeze, above bronze-green foliage. Autumn tints to the
leaves are an additional bonus.

Height × spread: 1m × 60cm/3 × 2ft

Soil: Best grown in fertile, moist but well drained neutral to acid soil.

Position: Well suited to a position in partial shade. Place as required
in the herbaceous or mixed border or appropriate garden situation.

Care: Cut down current season's growth completely to ground level in
autumn. Keep young plants well watered until established.

◐ ◇ LH ❄❄❄

Gladiolus byzantinus

The glowing magenta flowers of this hardy, cormous
perennial are a wondrous sight, particularly when massed
together, from late spring to early summer. The leaves are
mid-green, long, narrow and erect. Freely spreading when
conditions are to its liking, this plant makes an unusual
and dramatic addition to any border.

Height × spread: 60 × 8cm/2ft × 3in

Soil: Best grown in fertile, moist but well drained soil.

Position: Well suited to a position in full sun. Place as required in the
herbaceous or mixed border or appropriate garden situation.

Care: Cut down current season's growth completely to ground level
after flowering or in the early spring. Keep well watered until
established.

| ○ | ◊ | ❊❊❊ |

Gladiolus papilio

A highly unusual, frost-hardy cormous perennial which has a truly ethereal quality. A sea of strap-like, grey-green leaves is topped by flowers of a similar shade, flushed purple, from midsummer through until early autumn. A sophisticated plant for the late season border. Originating from South Africa, it benefits from winter protection in colder regions.

Height × spread: 75 × 8cm/2¹/₂ft × 3in

Soil: Best grown in fertile, moist but well drained soil.

Position: Well suited to a position in full sun. Place as required in the herbaceous or mixed border or appropriate garden situation.

Care: Cut down current season's growth completely to ground level after flowering or in the early spring. Keep well watered until established.

○ ◊ ❄❄

Helenium 'Moerheim Beauty': Helen's flower

Daisy-like flowerheads in a range of bronzy tints are produced on the tall stems of this perennial from midsummer to early autum. *H.* 'Golden Youth' is a deep yellow flowered form and other named varieties are also available, including the reddish-brown *H.* 'Bruno' and orange and yellow *H.* 'Septemberfuchs'. Reliably free flowering, this easy plant is a valuable provider of late season colour.

Height × spread: 1m × 60cm/3 × 2ft

Soil: Best grown in fertile, moist but well drained soil.

Position: Well suited to a position in full sun. Place as required in the herbaceous or mixed border or appropriate garden situation.

Care: Cut down current season's growth completely to ground level after flowering or in the early spring. Keep well watered until established.

○ ◊ ❋❋❋

Helleborus foetidus **'Wester Flisk'**: Stinking hellebore

A perennial of simple but striking beauty, this hellebore contributes a definite impact in any spring border. Brilliant red stems carry yellow-green flowers, flushed scarlet, in early spring above grey-green, deeply divided leaves. Look out for young seedlings to be found immediately around the parent plant. A sophisticated choice.

Height × spread: 45 × 45cm/1½ × 1½ft

Soil: Best grown in fertile, moist but well drained neutral to alkaline soil.

Position: Well suited to a position in sun or partial shade. Place as required in the herbaceous or mixed border or appropriate garden situation.

Care: Remove spent flowerheads and dead foliage in late winter before the emergence of new flowers. Enrich soil with garden compost or similar.

◐ | ◐ | ◊ | E | ✳✳✳

Hemerocallis 'Summer Wine': Day lily

Numerous named cultivars have been produced of this deservedly popular perennial. This form has magenta-pink flowers with dusky yellow stripes in summer. Although each flower lasts for just one day, as the common name suggests, it is immediately replaced by another over a prolonged period. For the sake of tidiness, it looks better if the dead flowers are cut off.

Height × spread: 60 × 60cm/2 × 2ft

Soil: Best grown in fertile, moist but well drained soil.

Position: Well suited to a position in sun or partial shade. Place as required in the herbaceous or mixed border or appropriate garden situation.

Care: Cut down current season's growth completely to ground level after flowering or in the early spring. Keep well watered until established.

○ ◑ | ◊ | ✽✽✽

Hosta 'Halcyon': Plantain lily

A compact, clump forming perennial with heart-shaped leaves of an unusual gunmetal blue. Lavender flowers are produced in summer but are of secondary interest to the eye-catching foliage of this versatile plant. Suitable for the border or in a container, it cannot fail to please. It is one of the neatest hostas, and ideal for a small garden.

Height × spread: 45 × 45cm/1 1/2 × 1 1/2ft

Soil: Best grown in fertile, moisture retentive soil which is not allowed to dry out.

Position: Well suited to a position in partial or full shade. Place as required in the herbaceous or mixed border or appropriate garden situation.

Care: Cut down current season's growth completely to ground level after flowering or in the early spring. Keep well watered until established.

◐ ● | ◊ | ❋❋❋

Imperata cylindrica 'Rubra': Japanese blood grass

An aristocrat amongst grasses, this slow, spreading perennial produces slender leaves of mid-green stained with blood-red towards the tips. Flower spikes of silver-white are carried in late summer. Position it to catch the late evening sun when it can appear breathtakingly beautiful.

Height × spread: 45 × 30cm/1½ × 1ft

Soil: Best grown in fertile, moisture retentive soil which is not allowed to dry out.

Position: Well suited to a position in sun or partial shade. Place as required in the herbaceous or mixed border or appropriate garden situation.

Care: Cut down current season's growth completely to ground level after flowering in the early spring. Keep well watered until established.

◐ ◑ | ◗ | ❋❋❋

Ipheion 'Rolf Fielder'

A frost hardy, bulbous perennial which forms a clump of narrow, strap-like leaves with scented, starry flowers of mid-blue in spring. Other forms of this plant can be found with paler and darker blue flowers. A pretty, dainty plant whose position needs to be marked as it dies away completely once the flowering period is finished. It can also be grown in a container.

Height × spread: 15 × 8cm/6 × 3in

Soil: Best grown in humus-rich, moist but well drained soil.

Position: Well suited to a position in full sun. Place as required in the herbaceous or mixed border or appropriate garden situation.

Care: Allow foliage and flowers to die down naturally. Apply a top dressing of garden compost or similar in autumn.

○ ◊ ❋❋

Iris graminea: Plum tart iris

An essential component of the quintessential country garden, the iris is a valuable and reliable garden plant. This species is a rhizomatous perennial producing violet-purple flowers set deep amongst the foliage in late spring and early summer. A close inspection of the flowers reveals an enticing perfume of cooked plums.

Height × spread: 30 × 30cm/1 × 1ft

Soil: Best grown in fertile, moist but well drained soil.

Position: Well suited to a position in sun or partial shade. Place as required in the herbaceous or mixed border or appropriate garden situation.

Care: Cut down current season's growth completely to ground level after flowering or in the early spring. Keep well watered until established.

◗◑ ◇ ❄❄❄

Iris 'Holden Clough'

A rhizomatous, beardless perennial iris with arching, semi-evergreen leaves. In late spring deep gold flowers, heavily netted with purple, are produced. The striking markings lift this plant out of the ordinary, setting it aside as a classic addition to the herbaceous border, or to a setting by the water garden. The leaves are greyish-green.

Height × spread: 1m × 60cm/3 × 2ft

Soil: For fertile, moist, or moist and well drained soil.

Position: Well suited to a position in sun or partial shade. Place as required in the herbaceous or mixed border or appropriate garden situation.

Care: Cut down flower stalks once flowering is finished. Remove any dead foliage to ground level in spring. Keep well watered until established.

Iris pallida 'Variegata'

A rhizomatous, bearded perennial iris with semi-evergreen leaves of clear green striped with pale yellow which are topped by flower stems carrying shiny, paper-like bracts. In late spring and early summer large, perfumed, light blue flowers with yellow beards are formed.

Height × spread: 1.2m × 60cm/4 × 2ft

Soil: Best grown in fertile, moist but well drained soil.

Position: Well suited to a position in sun or partial shade. Place as required in the herbaceous or mixed border or appropriate garden situation.

Care: Cut down flower stalks once flowering is finished. Remove any dead foliage to ground level in spring. Keep well watered until established.

◐◑ ◊ Semi-E ❄❄❄

Iris unguicularis: Algerian iris

The appearance of this evergreen, bearded iris in late winter and early spring is a lovely, welcome sight. Large, scented flowers of lavender-blue are carried over rush-like leaves providing that the rhizomes are planted in an open, sunny position and are provided with sharp drainage. Suitable for cultivation in a container. The form *I.u.* 'Mary Barnard' has violet flowers.

Height × spread: 60 × 30cm/2 × 1ft

Soil: Best grown in fertile, moist but well drained soil.

Position: Well suited to a position in full sun. Place as required in the herbaceous or mixed border or appropriate garden situation.

Care: Cut down flower stalks once flowering is finished. Remove any dead foliage to ground level in spring. Keep well watered until established.

◯ ◌ E ❋❋❋

Kirengeshoma palmata

Waxy, pale lemon flowers in late summer and early
autumn are the hallmark of this much sought-after
perennial. Finely cut mid to deep green leaves, not
dissimilar to those of a sycamore, provide interest all
through the season. When in flower, ensure an adequate
supply of moisture. A beautiful and interesting addition to
the late summer border in a shady position.

Height × spread: 1m × 75cm/3 × 2¹/₂ft

Soil: Best grown in humus-rich, moisture retentive lime free soil.

Position: Well suited to a position in partial shade. Place as required
in the herbaceous or mixed border or appropriate garden situation out
of the reach of cold winds.

Care: Cut down current season's growth completely to ground level in
autumn. Keep young plants well watered until established.

◑ ◔ LH ❊❊❊

Kniphofia caulescens: Red hot poker

Bold, torch-like flower spikes of burnt red and lemon soar above deeply serrated sword-like leaves of glaucous grey-green. Flowering from late summer to early autumn, this evergreen perennial makes a dramatic contrast to all other plants in the herbaceous border. It is particularly striking when planted in combination with the plum-coloured foliage of shrubs such as *Berberis* or *Cotinus*.

Height × spread: 1m × 60cm/3 × 2ft

Soil: Best grown in fertile, moist but well drained soil.

Position: Well suited to a position in full sun. Place as required in the herbaceous or mixed border or appropriate garden situation.

Care: Cut down flower stalks once flowering is finished. Remove any dead foliage to ground level in spring. Keep well watered until established.

| ○ | ◌ | E | ❋❋❋ |

Kniphofia 'Little Maid': Red hot poker

A deciduous perennial consisting of grassy leaves and narrow pokers of pale lemon and cream in late summer and early autumn. Many other forms of *Kniphofia* are available in shades ranging from red, orange and yellow to near white. They are of value for their late flowering and strong, architectural qualities, making vertical lines beside perennials of more horizontal growth.

Height × spread: 60 × 45cm/2 × 1¹/₂ft

Soil: Best grown in fertile, moist but well drained soil.

Position: Well suited to a position in sun or partial shade. Place as required in the herbaceous or mixed border or appropriate garden situation.

Care: Cut down current season's growth completely to ground level after flowering or in the early spring. Keep well watered until established.

◗◑ ◊ ✳✳✳

191

Lamium maculatum 'Wootton Pink': Dead nettle

A rhizomatous perennial of creeping habit bearing whorls of sugar-pink flowers above white splashed leaves in late spring and early summer. Excellent as ground cover to lighten up a dark corner of the herbaceous border and perfect in combination with all pastel coloured perennials.

Height × spread: 15 × 30cm/6in × 1ft

Soil: Best grown in fertile, moist but well drained soil.

Position: Well suited to a position in sun or partial shade. Place as required in the herbaceous or mixed border or appropriate garden situation.

Care: Cut down current season's growth completely to ground level after flowering or in the early spring. Keep well watered until established.

◑◑ ◇ ❋❋❋

Lilium regale: Regal lily

Highly scented, trumpet-shaped flowers of white, flushed with purple, are the principal attraction of this midsummer, bulbous perennial. Of all the lily cultivars, this species continues, deservedly, to find favour. An exotic addition to the herbaceous border or very suitable for growing in a pot, where a group of three or more, depending on the size of the container, will have impact.

Height: 60cm–2m/2–6ft depending on position.

Soil: Best grown in fertile, moist but well drained neutral to acidic soil.

Position: Well suited to a position in full sun. Place as required in the herbaceous or mixed border or appropriate garden situation.

Care: Cut down current season's growth completely to ground level after flowering or in the early spring. Keep well watered until established.

◯ ◌ ✽✽✽

193

Linum narbonense 'Heavenly Blue'

Grown en masse, this perennial makes a wonderful blue haze in early and midsummer when saucer-shaped flowers of intense violet-blue are carried on thin wiry stems above attractive grey-green leaves. Combines well with a wide range of other border perennials, particularly those in pastel shades. It tends to be short-lived and is on the borderline of being fully hardy.

Height × spread: 60 × 45cm/2 × 1½ft

Soil: Best grown in fertile, moist but well drained soil.

Position: Well suited to a position in full sun. Place as required in the herbaceous or mixed border or appropriate garden situation.

Care: Cut down current season's growth completely to ground level after flowering or in the early spring. Keep well watered until established.

◯ ◊ ❄❄❄ (borderline)

Lobelia 'Dark Crusader'

A hardy perennial with deep, maroon coloured leaves and flowers of dusky velvet-red in mid and late summer. The flower colour has a brilliant intensity which makes it an ideal component of any hot scheme in the herbaceous border. In cold areas apply a mulch to the crown over winter.

Height × spread: 75 × 30cm/2¹/₂ × 1ft

Soil: Best grown in fertile, moisture retentive soil which is not allowed to dry out.

Position: Well suited to a position in sun or partial shade. Place as required in the herbaceous or mixed border or appropriate garden situation.

Care: Cut down current season's growth completely to ground level after flowering or in the early spring. Keep well watered until established.

Lobelia siphilitica: Blue cardinal flower

Unusually for the lobelia family, this is a hardy perennial form. Clumps of pale green leaves carry stiff stems of bright blue, tubular flowers from late summer to mid-autumn. A reliable and versatile plant, it can offer late season colour wherever it is needed. The leaves are a light green and the plant makes a clump.

Height × spread: 60 × 30cm/2 × 1ft

Soil: Best grown in fertile, moisture retentive soil which is not allowed to dry out.

Position: Well suited to a position in sun or partial shade. Place as required in the herbaceous or mixed border or appropriate garden situation.

Care: Cut down current season's growth completely to ground level after flowering or in the early spring. Keep well watered until established.

◑◐ | ◊ | ❊❊❊

The brilliant scarlet flowers of this clump forming perennial make a spectacular sight in early and midsummer. The flowerheads are held high on stiff stems over basal leaves of mid-green. In some gardens it may need to be staked. Other forms of lychnis have flowers in shades of pink, purple or white, and a rare double form can be found.

Height × spread: 1m × 30cm/3 × 1ft

Soil: Best grown in fertile, moist but well drained soil.

Position: Well suited to a position in sun or partial shade. Place as required in the herbaceous or mixed border or appropriate garden situation.

Care: Cut down current season's growth completely to ground level after flowering or in the early spring. Keep well watered until established.

Lysichiton americanus: Skunk cabbage

An aquatic perennial with dramatic, large, shiny paddle-shaped leaves of mid-green and producing butter-yellow spathes in early spring. As its common name suggests, the smell from this plant can be unpleasant. Nevertheless, it is an eye-catching addition to the bog or pond garden where it combines well with other moisture loving perennials such as *Gunnera manicata*.

Height × spread: 1 × 1.2m/3 × 4ft

Soil: Best grown in fertile, damp to wet soil.

Position: Well suited to a position in sun or partial shade. Place at the margins of a pool or stream, in a bog garden or comparable situation.

Care: Cut down current season's growth to ground level in late autumn. Look out for seedling plants in spring.

○ ◐ | ◖ | ❄❄❄

Lysimachia clethroides: Loosestrife

This rhizomatous perennial, which is a superior form of loosestrife and altogether more garden worthy, flowers in summer. The racemes of saucer-shaped, white flowers, curving like a crook then arching upwards, combined with the grey-green foliage contribute to a somewhat ghostly appearance. An excellent choice for an all white garden.

Height × spread: 1m × 60cm/3 × 2ft

Soil: Best grown in fertile, moisture retentive soil which is not allowed to dry out.

Position: Well suited to a position in sun or partial shade. Place as required in the herbaceous or mixed border or appropriate garden situation.

Care: Cut down current season's growth completely to ground level after flowering or in the early spring. Keep well watered until established.

◐◑ ◖ ❋❋❋

Meconopsis cambrica: Welsh poppy

A deciduous perennial forming clumps of fresh green, serrated leaves over which lemon, yellow or orange poppy-like flowers are held on thin, wiry stems. Flowering from mid spring to late summer, the season can be extended still further by regular deadheading. A cheerful, dainty plant which self-seeds easily. There is also a double-flowered form, and one with orange flowers.

Height × spread: 45 × 30cm/1½ × 1ft

Soil: Best grown in fertile, moist but well drained soil.

Position: Well suited to a position in sun or partial shade. Place as required in the herbaceous or mixed border or appropriate garden situation.

Care: Cut down current season's growth completely to ground level after flowering or in the early spring. Keep well watered until established.

◯◑ ◇ ❄❄❄

Mertensia pulmonarioides: Virginia cowslip

Rarely seen, this spring flowering perennial makes a splendid impact in the early part of the season. Slate blue-green leaves are surmounted by flowers of an intense violet-blue. Unfortunately, slugs appear to be drawn to this plant which, in all other respects, is without fault. The leaves die down in summer, so the plant may need its position marked.

Height × spread: 45 × 30cm/1^{1}/$_{2}$ × 1ft

Soil: Best grown in fertile, moist but well drained soil.

Position: Well suited to a position in sun or partial shade. Place as required in the herbaceous or mixed border or appropriate garden situation.

Care: Cut down current season's growth completely to ground level after flowering or in the early spring. Keep well watered until established.

○ ◑ | △ | ✳✳✳

Monarda 'Cambridge Scarlet': Bergamot

Aromatic leaves of mid-green of this rhizomatous perennial provide an excellent background to the profusion of scarlet-crimson flowers produced from midsummer to early autumn. Many named varieties of bergamot are available including 'Croftway Pink', with china-pink flowers, and 'Prairie Night' whose flowers are a deep purple.

Height × spread: 1m × 45cm/3 × 1 1/2ft

Soil: Best grown in fertile, moist but well drained soil.

Position: Well suited to a position in sun or partial shade. Place as required in the herbaceous or mixed border or appropriate garden situation.

Care: Cut down current season's growth completely to ground level after flowering or in the early spring. Keep well watered until established.

Narcissus cyclamineus: Daffodil

The dainty, golden-yellow flowers of this bulbous perennial, appearing in the early spring, are an appealing sight when seen massed together as an underplanting to deciduous shrubs and trees. The tiny flowers with narrow, waisted trumpets add a certain sophistication to the spring garden and are a welcome change from the larger flower headed varieties.

Height: 15–20cm/6–8in

Soil: Best grown in fertile, moist but well drained, neutral to acid soil.

Position: Well suited to a position in sun or partial shade. Place as required in the herbaceous or mixed border or appropriate garden situation.

Care: Allow foliage and flowers to die down naturally. Apply a top dressing of garden compost or similar in autumn.

○ ◑ | △ | LH | ❄❄❄

Narcissus poeticus **var.** *recurvus*: Pheasant's eye

Heavenly scented, pure white flowers with yellow, red fringed centres make this bulbous perennial deservedly popular. Flowering from late spring to early summer, the pheasant's eye daffodils will, when planted in sufficient quantity, perfume an entire border in warm weather. No garden should be without this delightful bulb which should be planted deeply and left undisturbed.

Height: 30cm/1ft

Soil: Best grown in fertile, moist but well drained soil.

Position: Well suited to a position in sun or partial shade. Place as required in the herbaceous or mixed border or appropriate garden situation.

Care: Allow foliage and flowers to die down naturally. Apply a top dressing of garden compost or similar in autumn.

◐ ◑ | ◊ | ✳✳✳

Narcissus 'Thalia': Daffodil

With so many different varieties to choose from, selecting one of these bulbous perennials for the garden is not always easy. However, *N.* 'Thalia' is renowned for the constancy of its flower in mid-spring. Dark green foliage is topped by strong stems carrying two off-white, trumpet flowers of great beauty. A magical sight in dull weather.

Height: 30cm/1ft

Soil: Best grown in fertile, moist but well drained soil.

Position: Well suited to a position in sun or partial shade. Place as required in the herbaceous or mixed border or appropriate garden situation.

Care: Allow foliage and flowers to die down naturally. Apply a top dressing of garden compost or similar in autumn.

○ ◑ | ◊ | ❄❄❄

Nepeta 'Six Hills Giant': Catmint

This strong growing perennial produces clouds of aromatic grey-green leaves pierced by spikes of lavender-blue flowers in summer. An excellent 'filler' for the herbaceous border which is attractive to both butterflies and bees. Lovely, too, as an underplanting for old shrub roses or positioned to edge a path.

Height × **spread:** 1m × 60cm/3 × 2ft

Soil: Best grown in fertile, moist but well drained soil.

Position: Well suited to a position in sun or partial shade. Place as required in the herbaceous or mixed border or appropriate garden situation.

Care: Cut down current season's growth completely to ground level after flowering or in the early spring. Keep well watered until established.

◐◑ ◊ ✳✳✳

Nicotiana langsdorffii: Tobacco plant

A half-hardy annual which is noteworthy for its unusual, tubular lime-green flowers which are produced in summer. Although not as scented as other varieties of the tobacco plant, its colour and tall growing habit make it a distinctive and different choice for a summer bedding scheme. All *Nicotiana* are easily raised from seed sown in the spring.

Height × spread: 1m × 30cm/3 × 1ft

Soil: Best grown in fertile, moist but well drained soil.

Position: Well suited to a position in sun or partial shade. Place as required in the herbaceous or mixed border or appropriate garden situation.

Care: Deadhead regularly during the season to promote continuous flowering. Remove the entire plant after the first frost of winter.

◐◑ ◊ ❄

Nigella damascena: Love-in-a-mist

The feathery foliage of this annual, coupled with its dainty flowers of the palest blue in summer, make it a perfect choice for filling gaps in the herbaceous border. It combines well with a wide range of perennials and reliably self-seeds, but never to become a nuisance, to ensure plants for the next year. Other forms of this nigella have white, pink, dark rose or violet-blue flowers.

Height × spread: 45 × 23cm/1 1/2ft × 9in

Soil: Best grown in fertile, moist but well drained soil.

Position: Well suited to a position in full sun. Place as required in the herbaceous or mixed border or appropriate garden situation.

Care: Deadhead during the flowering season unless seeds or pods are wanted. Remove the entire plant after self-seeding has taken place.

❍ ◊ ❄❄❄

Omphalodes cappadocica 'Cherry Ingram': Navelwort

This compact, clump forming evergreen perennial is valuable for its deep blue, forget-me-not type flowers produced in early spring. Contrasting beautifully with spring bulbs, it is easy to grow and reliably free flowering. Other forms, such as *O. cappadocica* 'Alba' producing white flowers, are also available. Useful as a readily controlled form of ground cover.

Height × **spread:** 25 × 45cm/10in × 1 1/2ft

Soil: Best grown in humus-rich, moist but well drained soil.

Position: Well suited to a position in partial shade. Place as required in the herbaceous or mixed border or appropriate garden situation.

Care: Remove dead flowerheads and spent foliage throughout the season. Cut to ground level, if desired, in late winter. Keep well watered until established.

◑ ◊ E ❋❋❋

Origanum 'Kent Beauty': Marjoram

Valuable for their late and prolonged flowering season from late spring to autumn, all the marjorams make excellent border perennials. This particular variety has striking green and purple papery bracts carried on trailing stems. The flowers dry well. Useful for its tolerance of drought conditions, it is a splendid choice for the gravel garden.

Height × spread: 15 × 30cm/6in × 1ft

Soil: Best grown in poor, well drained alkaline soil.

Position: Well suited to a position in full sun. Place as required in the herbaceous or mixed border or appropriate garden situation.

Care: Cut down current season's growth completely to ground level after flowering or in the early spring. Keep well watered until established.

◐ ◊ ❄❄❄

Origanum laevigatum: Marjoram

From a mass of blue-green leaves are produced clouds of tiny tubular magenta-pink flowers with purplish bracts from late spring to autumn. An unusual perennial which adds a graceful charm to the late season herbaceous border. Easy, reliable and tolerant of poor conditions, it is both a flexible and worthwhile garden plant.

Height × spread: 60 × 45cm/2 × 1½ft

Soil: Best grown in poor, well drained alkaline soil.

Position: Well suited to a position in full sun. Place as required in the herbaceous or mixed border or appropriate garden situation.

Care: Cut down current season's growth completely to ground level after flowering or in the early spring. Keep well watered until established.

◔ ◊ ❋❋❋

Osteospermum 'Buttermilk': African daisy

This frost-hardy, evergreen sub-shrub, in habit not dissimilar to a perennial, is noted for its daisy-like flowers borne in profusion from late spring to autumn. This particular cultivar has dark-centred primrose-yellow flowers which are shaded bronze-yellow on the reverse. Other named forms cover a wide range of colours from purple through pink to white.

Height × spread: 60 × 60cm/2 × 2ft

Soil: Best grown in fertile, moist but well drained soil.

Position: Well suited to a position in full sun. Place as required in the herbaceous or mixed border or appropriate garden situation.

Care: Deadhead throughout the growing season. Cut back stems to new shoots in spring. Keep well watered until established.

◯ ◊ E ❋❋

Paeonia lactiflora 'Bowl of Beauty': Peony

Unusual, anemone-form flowers of deep pink with prominent creamy centres are produced in early summer, together with leaves of mid-green often colouring in autumn, by this perennial form of peony. Resenting disturbance, new plants may take time to settle and it may well be three years before flowering commences.

Height × spread: 1 × 1m/3 × 3ft

Soil: Best grown in humus-rich, moist but well drained soil.

Position: Well suited to a position in sun or partial shade. Place as required in the herbaceous or mixed border or appropriate garden situation.

Care: Cut down current season's growth completely to ground level after flowering or in the early spring. Keep well watered until established.

Paeonia lactiflora 'Monsieur Jules Elie': Peony

Aristocrats of the herbaceous border, no other plants compare with the fulsome beauty of peonies. This perennial form has dark green leaves and large double flowers of deep silvery-pink in early summer. These heads are so heavy that they will require some support. Long-lived, this plant will continue to give pleasure for season after season.

Height × spread: 1 × 1m/3 × 3ft

Soil: Best grown in humus-rich, moist but well drained soil.

Position: Well suited to a position in sun or partial shade. Place as required in the herbaceous or mixed border or appropriate garden situation.

Care: Cut down current season's growth completely to ground level after flowering or in the early spring. Keep well watered until established.

○ ◑ | ◌ | ✱✱✱

Papaver orientale 'Charming'

Fleetingly beautiful, this perennial poppy has large, open flowers of blush lilac-pink with black centres, each petal splashed with charcoal, in late spring and early summer. It is best combined with later flowering perennials which can be positioned to conceal the dying foliage of the poppy. Other oriental poppies have flowers of white, scarlet, orange or plum, often marked with black.

Height × spread: 60 × 60cm/2 × 2ft

Soil: Best grown in fertile, moist but well drained soil.

Position: Well suited to a position in full sun. Place as required in the herbaceous or mixed border or appropriate garden situation.

Care: Cut down current season's growth completely to ground level after flowering or in the early spring. Keep well watered until established.

◐ ◊ ✻✻✻

Penstemon 'Apple Blossom'

A semi-evergreen perennial with narrow leaves of mid-green and carrying tubular flowers of pale pink with white throats from midsummer to mid-autumn. Many named cultivars of this reliable mainstay of the summer herbaceous border are available in colours ranging from deepest purple through reds, pinks and lilac to white. Most are easily raised from cuttings taken in late summer.

Height × spread: 60 × 60cm/2 × 2ft

Soil: Best grown in fertile, moist but well drained soil.

Position: Well suited to a position in full sun. Place as required in the herbaceous or mixed border or appropriate garden situation.

Care: Cut down current season's growth completely to ground level after flowering or in the early spring. Keep well watered until established.

◐ ◊ Semi-E ❄❄❄

216

Phlox carolina 'Bill Baker'

It is difficult to commend this perennial phlox too highly.
From a base of glossy, dark green foliage a mass of
magenta pink flowers are produced in profusion over a
prolonged period throughout the summer. An essential
component of any herbaceous scheme, regular
deadheading will ensure continuous flowering.

Height × spread: 45 × 30cm/1¹/₂ × 1ft

Soil: Best grown in fertile, moist but well drained soil.

Position: Well suited to a position in sun or partial shade. Place as
required in the herbaceous or mixed border or appropriate garden
situation.

Care: Cut down current season's growth completely to ground level after
flowering or in the early spring. Keep well watered until established.

◯ ◑ │ ◌ │ ❋❋❋

Phlox divaricata 'May Breeze'

An unusual, semi-evergreen perennial form of phlox of low growing habit and which produces clouds of white starry flowers, flushed with pink, in early summer. Delicately scented, it makes a highly attractive front of border plant which, if deadheaded regularly, will be reliably free flowering. It is also as well suited to growing in containers as in the borders.

Height × spread: 30 × 45cm/1 × 1 1/2ft

Soil: Best grown in fertile, moist but well drained soil.

Position: Well suited to a position in partial shade. Place as required in the herbaceous or mixed border or appropriate garden situation.

Care: Remove dead flowerheads throughout the growing season. Cut back stems to new shoots in spring. Keep well watered until established.

◐ ◊ Semi-E ❄❄❄

Phlox paniculata 'Fujiyama'

The tall growing, late flowering phlox are, by tradition, one of the mainstays of the herbaceous border. This particular variety has pure white, scented flowers produced in abundance in summer and early autumn. A dramatic and eye-catching perennial which is worthy of inclusion in any garden scheme.

Height × spread: 75 × 60cm/2¹/₂ × 2ft

Soil: Best grown in fertile, moist but well drained soil.

Position: Well suited to a position in sun or partial shade. Place as required in the herbaceous or mixed border or appropriate garden situation.

Care: Cut down current season's growth completely to ground level after flowering or in the early spring. Keep well watered until established.

◐◑ ◊ ❄❄❄

Phlox paniculata 'Norah Leigh'

The attraction of this late summer flowering perennial phlox is not simply its pale pinky-lilac flowers but also its leaves which are prettily variegated in pale cream and green. An additional bonus is its sweet scent which is more heavily defined if grown in full sun and in an enclosed space.

Height × spread: 75 × 60cm/2¹/₂ × 2ft

Soil: Best grown in fertile, moist but well drained soil.

Position: Well suited to a position in full sun. Place as required in the herbaceous or mixed border or appropriate garden situation.

Care: Cut down current season's growth completely to ground level after flowering or in the early spring. Keep well watered until established.

◐ ◊ ❄❄❄

Phormium tenax

This frost hardy perennial is of value for the way in which it provides a contrast of form and texture in the garden. Over stiff, upright evergreen leaves of dark green, blue-green on the undersides, are produced tubular, dull red flowers rising high on thick, stout stems in summer. An unusual subject for a large container where it will be guaranteed to create an impact. Other forms are obtainable with brightly coloured or purple-bronze leaves.

Height × spread: 4 × 2m/13 × 6ft

Soil: Best grown in fertile, well drained soil.

Position: Well suited to a position in full sun. Place as required in the herbaceous or mixed border or appropriate garden situation.

Care: Remove spent flowers and any dead leaves to keep the plant looking good. Apply a mulch in winter for added protection.

| ○ | ◊ | E | ❄❄ |

Polemonium **'Lambrook Mauve'**: Jacob's ladder

Clumps of divided, fresh green leaves carry pretty cup-shaped flowers of lilac-blue with yellow centres in late spring and early summer. An attractive and easy, well-behaved perennial which associates well with other plants sharing similar pastel colourings. It is a welcome change from the more widely grown and taller *P. caeruleum*.

Height × spread: 45 × 45cm/1$\frac{1}{2}$ × 1$\frac{1}{2}$ft

Soil: Best grown in fertile, moist but well drained soil.

Position: Well suited to a position in sun or partial shade. Place as required in the herbaceous or mixed border or appropriate garden situation.

Care: Cut down current season's growth completely to ground level after flowering or in the early spring. Keep well watered until established.

| ◖◑ | ◊ | ❋❋❋ |

Polygonatum* × *hybridum: Solomon's seal

The arching stems of this perennial carry ribbed leaves of mid-green with cream and green, bell-shaped flowers in late spring. A dramatic, architectural plant which readily forms bold clumps. The flowers are followed by small, blue-black fruits. Other forms are available, some of which are tiny replicas of this plant, others with variegated foliage. It is prone to attacks from sawfly larvae.

Height × spread: 1.2m × 30cm/4 × 1ft

Soil: Best grown in fertile, moist but well drained soil.

Position: Well suited to a position in partial shade. Place as required in the herbaceous or mixed border or appropriate garden situation.

Care: Cut down current season's growth completely to ground level in autumn. Keep young plants well watered until established.

◑ ◊ ❄❄❄

Primula florindae: Giant cowslip

This deciduous perennial forms rosettes of toothed, fresh green leaves over which are carried clusters of scented, tubular, sulphur-yellow flowers on stout stems in summer. As the common name suggests, the plant closely resembles a large, multi-flowering cowslip and gives a dramatic impact when planted in bold groups. It looks well beside a water garden.

Height × spread: 1 × 1m/3 × 3ft

Soil: Best grown in fertile, moisture retentive soil which is not allowed to dry out.

Position: Well suited to a position in full sun. Place as required in the herbaceous or mixed border or appropriate garden situation.

Care: Cut down current season's growth completely to ground level after flowering or in the early spring. Keep well watered until established.

◑ ◐ ❄❄❄

If only one primula could be chosen, then it would have to be this one if only for its curiosity value. This evergreen perennial possesses dark bronze, finely toothed leaves over which are carried pale purple-pink flowers with yellow centres in spring. Slow to increase, it is very suitable for inclusion in the rock garden or the alpine house.

Height × spread: 12 × 25cm/5 × 10in

Soil: Best grown in fertile, moisture retentive soil which is not allowed to dry out. Prefers neutral to acidic conditions.

Position: Well suited to a position in partial shade. Place as required in the herbaceous or mixed border or appropriate garden situation.

Care: Remove spent flowers after flowering and any dead leaves. Apply a mulch of garden compost or similar over winter.

◑ ◐ E ❄❄❄

Primula viallii

The poker-like spikes of scarlet and magenta-pink flowers make this an eye-catching perennial. Flowering in summer above rosettes of mid-green, slightly hairy leaves, it is a most unusual form of primula which, when grown well, gives great impact to the flower border. Associates well with water at the pool or streamside. It is inclined to be short-lived.

Height × spread: 30–60 × 30cm/1–2 × 1ft

Soil: Best grown in fertile, moisture retentive soil which is not allowed to dry out. Prefers neutral to acidic conditions.

Position: Well suited to a position in partial shade. Place as required in the herbaceous or mixed border or appropriate garden situation.

Care: Cut down current season's growth completely to ground level after flowering or in the early spring. Keep well watered until established.

◑ ◊ LH ❅❅❅

Pulmonaria officinalis '**Sissinghurst White**': Lungwort

Valuable for their late winter and early spring flowers, all of the pulmonarias are well worth growing for leaf as well as for flower. This particular form is a semi-evergreen perennial of clump forming habit with leaves of mid-green heavily spotted with white. Tiny, white funnel-shaped flowers are produced in abundance throughout the spring.

Height × spread: 30 × 45cm/1 × 1¹/₂ft

Soil: Best grown in fertile, moisture retentive soil which is not allowed to dry out.

Position: Well suited to a position in partial shade or full shade. Place as required in the herbaceous or mixed border or appropriate garden situation.

Care: Remove spent flowers after flowering and any dead leaves. Keep well watered until established.

◑ ● | ◔ | Semi-E | ❅❅❅

Pulsatilla vulgaris var. rubra: Pasque flower

The attractively cut, fern-like foliage of this perennial carries large, bell-shaped wine-red flowers in spring to be followed, later in the season, with striking, silky seedheads which are both long lasting and an attraction in their own right. Its compact growth makes this plant very suitable for any number of garden situations, including the rockery.

Height × spread: 20 × 20cm/8 × 8in

Soil: Best grown in fertile, light and well drained soil.

Position: Well suited to a position in full sun. Place as required in the herbaceous or mixed border or appropriate garden situation.

Care: Cut down current season's growth completely to ground level after flowering or in the early spring. Keep well watered until established.

Ranunculus ficaria 'Brazen Hussy': Buttercup

A startlingly showy perennial which is definitely not for those who favour only muted tones. Shiny, chocolate-brown foliage provides a background to glossy, sulphur-yellow flowers in early spring. Summer dormant, this spectacular plant erupts almost without warning to herald the start of a new gardening year. Left to its own devices it will gradually colonize an area.

Height × spread: 5 × 30cm/2in × 1ft

Soil: Best grown in fertile, moist but well drained soil.

Position: Well suited to a position in partial or full shade. Place as required in the herbaceous or mixed border or appropriate garden situation.

Care: Allow foliage and flowers to die down naturally. Apply a top dressing of garden compost or similar in autumn.

◐ ● | △ | ❋❋❋

Rheum palmatum: Chinese rhubarb

An ornamental foliage plant which carries imposing flower panicles of creamy-green to deep red, starry flowers in early summer. A rhizomatous perennial with huge leaves of deep green, the undersides of which are crimson-red, it provides a bold statement in the border. Given space and damp conditions, this plant is capable of tremendous growth during the season.

Height × spread: 2.4 × 2m/8 × 6ft

Soil: Best grown in fertile, moisture retentive soil which is not allowed to dry out.

Position: Well suited to a position in sun or partial shade. Place as required in the border or at the margins of a pond or stream.

Care: Cut down current season's growth completely to ground level after flowering or in the early spring. Keep well watered until established.

◐◑ ◊ ❋❋❋

Rudbeckia var. *sullivantii* 'Goldsturm': Coneflower

Unrivalled for its flowering capacity from late summer to mid-autumn, this clump forming perennial is a must for any situation requiring massed colour at the close of the season. Large yellow-ochre, daisy-like flowerheads with black, cone-like centres are produced in profusion over a long period. Team with purple *Verbena bonariensis* for a striking effect.

Height × spread: 60 × 45cm/2 × 1 1/2ft

Soil: Best grown in fertile, moist but well drained soil.

Position: Well suited to a position in sun or partial shade. Place as required in the herbaceous or mixed border or appropriate garden situation.

Care: Cut down current season's growth completely to ground level after flowering or in the early spring. Keep well watered until established.

◐◑ △ ❋❋❋

This form of salvia is a woody based perennial with woolly grey leaves carrying racemes of lilac-blue flowers in late spring and again in early autumn. Free flowering and with aromatic foliage, this plant is a valuable and reliable border perennial particularly suited to a gravel or a Mediterranean garden. It is on the edge of being fully hardy.

Height × spread: 45 × 60cm/1$^1/_2$ × 2ft

Soil: Best grown in fertile, moist but well drained soil.

Position: Well suited to a position in full sun. Place as required in the herbaceous or mixed border or appropriate garden situation.

Care: Cut back or prune out any old or damaged stems in late winter. Keep well watered until established. Propagate from cuttings.

○ ◊ ❄❄❄ (borderline)

Salvia patens: Sage

Hooded, midnight blue flowers are produced continuously by this frost hardy, tuberous perennial from midsummer to mid-autumn. A hauntingly beautiful plant which combines readily with a wide range of border perennials from pastel shades to deeper tones. Well worth any difficulty of over-wintering. A choice plant to include in any garden scheme.

Height × spread: 60 × 45cm/2 × 1½ft

Soil: Best grown in fertile, moist but well drained soil.

Position: Well suited to a position in full sun. Place as required in the herbaceous or mixed border or appropriate garden situation.

Care: Either apply a heavy mulch in winter in cold areas or lift, pot and protect from frost. In warmer situations cut down current season's growth in early spring. Propagate from cuttings.

◯ ◇ ❄❄

Salvia uliginosa: Sage

A frost hardy, rhizomatous perennial which forms clumps of toothed, mid-green leaves producing long, airy wands of stems topped by clear, light blue flowers in late summer and mid-autumn. Very late in its flowering habit, it is a challenge to see the flowers before early frosts cut the plants down.

Height × spread: 2 × 1m/6 × 3ft

Soil: Best grown in fertile, moist but well drained soil.

Position: Well suited to a position in full sun. Place as required in the herbaceous or mixed border or appropriate garden situation.

Care: Either apply a heavy mulch in winter in cold areas or lift, pot and protect from frost. In warmer situations cut down current season's growth in early spring. Propagate from cuttings.

◐ ◇ ✳✳

Bleached double white flowers are produced in spring above pale green, lobed leaves. The rhizomes of this perennial when cut ooze red sap giving rise to the common name of bloodroot. Valuable for the intensity of its flowers, it is, sadly, all too fleeting. A very rare pink form does exist but is seldom seen. There is also a single white form.

Height × **spread:** 15 × 30cm/6in × 1ft

Soil: Best grown in humus-rich, moist but well drained soil.

Position: Well suited to a position in partial shade. Place as required in the herbaceous or mixed border or appropriate garden situation.

Care: Allow foliage and flowers to die down naturally. Apply a top dressing of garden compost or similar in autumn.

◑ ◊ ✳✳✳

Scabiosa caucasica: Scabious

A charming perennial which is capable of thriving in the poorest of conditions. Papery, lilac-coloured flowers are produced in early and midsummer over a long period if continually deadheaded. Good in combination with all pastel shades, the delicate tracery of its foliage contrasts beautifully with the more substantial nature of its flowerheads. There are also named white forms obtainable.

Height × spread: 60 × 60cm/2 × 2ft

Soil: Best grown in fertile, moist but well drained soil.

Position: Well suited to a position in full sun. Place as required in the herbaceous or mixed border or appropriate garden situation.

Care: Cut down current season's growth completely to ground level after flowering or in the early spring. Keep well watered until established.

◯ ◌ ✽✽✽

Sidalcea 'Reverend Page Roberts': False mallow

This attractive perennial carries small hollyhock-like flowers of a pale rose-pink over basal leaves of mid-green in summer. The pink shade is somewhat quieter than the vibrant tones of the more widely grown *S.* 'Party Girl'. A very worthwhile addition to the herbaceous border. It will benefit from having the spent flower-heads cut off.

Height × spread: 1m × 45cm/3 × 1½ft

Soil: Best grown in fertile, moist neutral to acidic but well drained soil.

Position: Well suited to a position in full sun. Place as required in the herbaceous or mixed border or appropriate garden situation.

Care: Remove spent flowers and any dead leaves to keep the plant looking good. Cut down current season's growth completely to ground level in autumn.

○ ◊ LH ❋❋❋

Smilacina racemosa: False Solomon's seal

The pointed, glossy, dark green veined leaves of this perennial provide an excellent contrast to the panicles of pale cream flowers produced in spring. These flowers emit a heavy, sweet, penetrating scent. In autumn, the leaves turn a golden-yellow and the flowers mature to green fruits, ripening to glossy red. A good choice wherever a long season of interest is required.

Height × spread: 1m × 60cm/3 × 2ft

Soil: Best grown in fertile, moist but well drained soil.

Position: Well suited to a position in partial shade. Place as required in the herbaceous or mixed border or appropriate garden situation.

Care: Cut down current season's growth completely to ground level in autumn. Keep young plants well watered until established.

◑ ◊ ❋❋❋

Stachys macrantha: Betony

The deep green, crinkly, veined leaves of this upright perennial carry spikes of hooded pink-purple flowers on tall stems in summer. An attractive foliage plant which can be guaranteed to flower reliably well whatever the seasonal weather. Other forms of stachys, such as *S. byzantina* 'Silver Carpet' have very different woolly grey foliage which provides an interesting foil to many other perennials.

Height × spread: 60 × 30cm/2 × 1ft

Soil: Best grown in fertile, moist but well drained soil.

Position: Well suited to a position in sun or partial shade. Place as required in the herbaceous or mixed border or appropriate garden situation.

Care: Cut down current season's growth completely to ground level after flowering or in the early spring. Keep well watered until established.

○ ◑ | ◊ | ✳✳✳

Thalictrum aquilegiifolium: Meadow rue

Clouds of fluffy pink, purple or white flowers are produced by this perennial on stiff, thin stems above aquilegia-like leaves of mid-green in early summer. Regular deadheading will produce continuous flowering over a long period but, when flowers are left to develop, then they will gently seed about, producing plants which usually have mauve flowers.

Height × spread: 1m × 45cm/3 × 1½ft

Soil: Best grown in humus-rich, moist but well drained soil.

Position: Well suited to a position in partial shade. Place as required in the herbaceous or mixed border or appropriate garden situation.

Care: Cut down current season's growth completely to ground level after flowering or in the early spring. Keep well watered until established.

◐ ◇ ❄❄❄

Thermopsis montana

Butter-yellow, lupin-like flowers contrast beautifully with the glaucous blue-green leaves of this seldom seen perennial. Flowering in late spring and early summer, it spreads well given good growing conditions. Well after the flowers have been deadheaded, the foliage will last for many months and provide an interesting contrast of form to later flowering perennials.

Height × spread: 75 × 75cm/2^1/$_2$ × 2^1/$_2$ft

Soil: Best grown in fertile, moist but well drained soil.

Position: Well suited to a position in sun or partial shade. Place as required in the herbaceous or mixed border or appropriate garden situation.

Care: Cut down current season's growth completely to ground level after flowering or in the early spring. Keep well watered until established.

◐ ◑ | ◊ | ❋❋❋

Trillium grandiflorum 'Roseum': Wake robin

Although rare and seldom seen, this clump-forming perennial is a most appealing plant producing funnel-shaped flowers of clear sugar-pink in late spring and early summer. Leaves of deep green cluster in groups of three around the flowerheads. Delicate in appearance only, this is a charming plant which is well worth seeking out. Equal in beauty, the white *T. grandiflorum* is widely available.

Height × spread: 45 × 30cm/1 $^1/_2$ × 1ft

Soil: Best grown in humus-rich, moist but well drained acidic to neutral soil.

Position: Well suited to a position in partial or full shade. Place in the herbaceous or mixed border or appropriate garden situation.

Care: Cut down current season's growth completely to ground level in autumn. Keep young plants well watered until established.

◑ ● ◊ LH ❄❄❄

Tulipa 'Black Parrot': Tulip

A bulbous perennial producing near black, fringed flowers in the late spring. Belonging to the Parrot group of tulips, this particular form makes for an exciting choice of bulb. Contrasting wonderfully with the pale green foliage, the single, deeply coloured flowers are held upright on thick, long stems. Plant in generous numbers for a real effect.

Height: 60cm/2ft

Soil: Best grown in fertile, moist but well drained soil.

Position: Well suited to a position in sun or partial shade. Place as required in the herbaceous or mixed border or appropriate garden situation.

Care: Allow foliage and flowers to die down naturally. Apply a top dressing of garden compost or similar in autumn.

◐ ◑ | ◊ | ✳✳✳

Tulipa sprengeri: Tulip

Stylishly elegant, this species bulbous perennial belongs to the Miscellaneous group of tulips. Stiff, slender stems hold high above the foliage single flowers of crimson-red with pale ochre markings at the base in early summer. Amongst the last tulips to flower, *T. sprengeri* is easily propagated from seed and will gradually increase by self-seeding if flowerheads are left to mature.

Height: 45cm/1¹/₂ft

Soil: Best grown in fertile, moist but well drained soil.

Position: Well suited to a position in sun or partial shade. Place as required in the herbaceous or mixed border or appropriate garden situation.

Care: Allow foliage and flowers to die down naturally. Apply a top dressing of garden compost or similar in autumn.

○ ◑ | ◊ | ✳ ✳ ✳

Tulipa 'Spring Green': Tulip

Belonging to the Viridiflora group, this bulbous perennial tulip is attractive and reliable. Bowl-shaped, single flowers of creamy-white, flashed with mid-green markings, appear in late spring. Stout stems enable the flowerheads to withstand strong winds well, a valuable asset in the early part of the growing season. Plant in large groups rather than singly.

Height: 45cm/1 ¹/₂ft

Soil: Best grown in fertile, moist but well drained soil.

Position: Well suited to a position in sun or partial shade. Place as required in the herbaceous or mixed border or appropriate garden situation.

Care: Allow foliage and flowers to die down naturally. Apply a top dressing of garden compost or similar in autumn.

◐◑ ◊ ❄❄❄

Somewhat surprisingly this unusual and interesting perennial is seldom seen in gardens. In mid and late spring, hanging tubular flowers of clear yellow are carried among newly emerged, downward pointing leaves of mid-green. It is an ideal candidate for a woodland garden, to grow among shrubs or, indeed, any shady situation out of the reach of full sun.

Height × spread: 30 × 30cm/1 × 1ft

Soil: Best grown in humus-rich, moist but well drained soil. Prefers acidic to neutral conditions.

Position: Well suited to a position in partial shade. Place as required in the herbaceous or mixed border or appropriate garden situation.

Care: Cut down current season's growth completely to ground level after flowering or in the early spring. Keep well watered until established.

◐ ◌ LH ❋❋❋

Prized as a dramatic foliage plant, this clump forming perennial is a spectacular sight when fully mature. From deep green, pleated leaves erupts a tall flower spike of near black flowers, the backs of which are striped green, in mid and late summer. A strange, slightly sinister plant which is guaranteed to give a bold effect to any border.

Height × spread: 1m × 60cm/3 × 2ft

Soil: Best grown in humus-rich, moist but well drained soil.

Position: Well suited to a position in partial shade. Place as required in the herbaceous or mixed border or appropriate garden situation.

Care: Cut down current season's growth completely to ground level after flowering or in the early spring. Keep well watered until established.

◐ ◊ ❄❄❄

Verbena bonariensis

Although a frost-hardy and short-lived perennial, no-one should dismiss this elegantly beautiful plant. Rigid, head high, branching stems carry a myriad of tiny, neon-lilac flowers which appear to glow from midsummer through to mid-autumn. An excellent plant to employ to come up through earlier flowering perennials. Allow to self-seed to ensure a continuous supply of new plants.

Height × spread: 2m × 45cm/6 × 1 1/2ft

Soil: Best grown in fertile, moist but well drained soil.

Position: Well suited to a position in full sun. Place as required in the herbaceous or mixed border or appropriate garden situation.

Care: Cut down current season's growth completely to ground level after flowering or in the early spring. Keep well watered until established.

Veronica gentianoides 'Tissington White': Speedwell

Where good ground cover is needed, then this attractive carpeting perennial is an excellent choice. Cup-shaped white flowers with just a hint of blue are produced in early summer above rosettes of lance-shaped, deep green leaves. A form with variegated leaves is also available, although this is less vigorous in growth.

Height × **spread:** 45 × 45cm/1 1/2 × 1 1/2ft

Soil: Best grown in fertile, moist but well drained soil.

Position: Well suited to a position in full sun. Place as required in the herbaceous or mixed border or appropriate garden situation.

Care: Cut down current season's growth completely to ground level after flowering or in the early spring. Keep well watered until established.

| ○ | ◊ | ✸✸✸ |

Veronica peduncularis 'Georgia Blue': Speedwell

Amazing for its capacity to flower intermittently all year round, this mat-forming perennial is an essential component of the herbaceous border. Deep Oxford-blue, saucer-shaped flowers are produced prolifically in early spring to summer and occasionally in autumn and winter. The shiny, mid-green leaves become tinged purple with age.

Height × spread: 45 × 30cm/1½ × 1ft

Soil: Best grown in fertile, moist but well drained soil.

Position: Well suited to a position in full sun. Place as required in the herbaceous or mixed border or appropriate garden situation.

Care: Cut down current season's growth completely to ground level after flowering or in the early spring. Keep well watered until established.

◑ ◊ ❄❄❄

Viola labradorica: Labrador violet

Remarkable for its purple tinged foliage, this semi-evergreen perennial makes a useful ground cover plant, particularly in dry partial shade. Lilac-purple flowers are produced in spring and summer to make an attractive contrast with the dark foliage. Freely self-seeding, it multiples vigorously and can become something of a nuisance in an inappropriate setting if left unattended.

Height × **spread:** 8cm/3in × indefinite spread

Soil: Best grown in fertile, moist but well drained soil.

Position: Well suited to a position in sun or partial shade. Place as required in the herbaceous or mixed border or appropriate garden situation.

Care: Remove unwanted seedlings. Or to prevent self-sowing, trim off spent flowers.

○ ◑ │ ◊ │ Semi-E │ ❄❄❄

Pure white, arum-type flowers are produced above glossy, dark green leaves from late spring to midsummer. A frost-hardy perennial, its crowns need winter protection to avoid frost damage. However, the extra care is well worth the strikingly beautiful display that this plant gives. It is particularly stunning when grown near water.

Height × **spread:** 60 × 60cm/2 × 2ft

Soil: Best grown in fertile, moisture retentive soil which is not allowed to dry out.

Position: Well suited to a position in full sun. Place as required in the herbaceous or mixed border or may be grown as a marginal aquatic.

Care: Cut down current season's growth completely to ground level in the early spring. Apply a heavy mulch in winter in cold areas.

○ ◊ ❋❋/❋❋❋

Index of Common Names

A

African daisy. See *Arctotis × hybrida* 125

African daisy. See *Osteospermum* 212

African lily. See *Agapanthus* 116

Algerian iris. See *Iris unguicularis* 188

Angelica tree. See *Aralia elata* 19

Avens. See *Geum* 175

B

Barberry. See *Berberis thunbergii* 23

Barrenwort. See *Epimedium × youngianum* 160

Bear's breeches. See *Acanthus spinosissimus* 113

Beauty berry. See *Callicarpa bodineri* var. *giraldii* 29

Beauty bush. See *Kolkwitzia amabalis* 78

Beech. See *Fagus sylvatica* 60

Bellflower. See *Campanula* species 134–135

Bellwort. See *Uvularia grandiflora* 246

Bergamot. See *Monarda* 202

Betony. See *Stachys macrantha* 239

Black false hellebore. See *Veratrum nigrum* 247

Black gum. See *Nyssa sylvatica* 90

Bleeding heart. See *Dicentra* 154

Bloodroot. See *Sanguinaria canadensis* 235

Blue cardinal flower. See *Lobelia siphilitica* 196

Blue spiraea. See *Caryopteris* 31

Broom. See *Cytisus × kewensis* 50

Bugle. See *Ajuga reptans* 117

Burning bush. See *Dictamnus albus* var. *purpureus* 155

Buttercup. See *Ranunculus ficaria* 229

Butterfly bush. See *Buddleja* species 25–26

C

Cabbage palm. See *Cordyline australis* 44

Calico bush. See *Kalmia latifolia* 76

California lilac. See *Ceanothus* 32

Calla lily. See *Zantedeschia aethiopica* 252

Cape figwort. See *Phygelius aequalis* 96

Catmint. See *Nepeta* 206

Chilean fire bush. See *Embothrium coccineum* 56

Chinese rhubarb. See *Rheum palmatum* 230

Chocolate flower. See *Cosmos atrosanguineus* 143

Columbine. See *Aquilegia* 124

Cone flower. See *Echinacea* 158–159

Cone flower. See *Rudbeckia* var. *sullivantii* 231

Crab apple. See *Malus hupehensis* 86

Cranesbill. See *Geranium* 173–174